Katsuyuki Kamei

Risk Management
- Basic Theory and Case -

Kansai University Press

© 2019 by Katsuyuki Kamei

All rights reserved. No part of this publication may be reproduced or transmitted in any form or by any means, electronic, or mechanical, including photocopy, recording, or any information storage or retrieval system, without permission in writing from publisher.

Kansai University Press
3-3-35 Yamate-cho, Suita-shi,
Osaka 564-8680, Japan.

Printed in Japan by Ishikawa Special Express Binding Co., Ltd., Osaka, Japan.

ISBN 978-4-87354-706-0　C3034

Published under the regulation of publication grants
for the achievement of research of the
Kansai University

Risk Management
- Basic Theory and Case -

Introduction

Risk management consists of a series of actions to list out all possible risks, evaluate their influences, and reduce or avoid the losses. (Hayashi and Kamei, 2018)[1]. In one word, it is a decision on risk treatment.

We start this book by showing major points of risk management as a decision making.[2]

Major Points of Risk Management from a Viewpoint of Decisiveness

1) Decision in a process - 3 'tei's
   Tokutei, identification (to find)→*Sohtei*, estimation (to anticipate) →*Kettei*, decision (to determine a countermeasure)
2) Decision to optimize the risk balance
   Taking a risk to optimize the risk balance for increased benefit and reduced loss
3) Decision with consideration for the worst scenario
   Considering backwards from the worst scenario enables the ability to find a means of preventing the worst scenario
4) Decision based on two Cs
   Communication: discussion of the risk treatments for mutual understanding
   Coordination: arrangement of the risk treatments for construction of system
5) C, S and R of risk management
   Choice: decision to determine a measure for the risk
   Someday/Somewhere: decision to be alert for encounters of disasters someday, somewhere
   Respect: resolution to respect workers who strive for safety management at work sites
6) Resolution learned through lessons of failure or disaster
7) Decision to respect what to maintain based not on a short-time interest, but on a long-term point of view

8) Decision to put a priority on physical and mental health
9) Risk management decisions for small and medium-sized enterprises
   To successfully start a business, and to avoid the risk of bankruptcy
10) Decision regarding insurance
    (a) To determine whether or not to insure
    (b) To determine what insurance to be taken if insured
    (c) To determine what insurance company to use
    (d) To determine contractual coverage, considering insurable contingency (cases to be paid insurance money) and exclusion of payment (cases not to be paid insurance money)

* Supplementary explanation: determining what is important for the risk management in this modern society
• Social risk management: local community and coordination
• Intangible things: brand name, reputation, and mental health

Note:

1) Yoshinari Hayashi and Katsuyuki Kamei, "Risk Management", Seiji Abe, Mamoru Ozawa, Yoshiaki Kawata ed., *Science of Societal Safety Living at Times of Risks and Disasters*, Springer, 2018, Chapter 11, p.121.
2) From the Introduction of Katsuyuki Kamei, *Risk Management from a Viewpoint of Decisiveness*, ("*Ketsudanryoku ni miru Risk Management*"), Minerva Publishing, 2017, pp.2-22.

Contents

Introduction i

Chapter 1 Basic Concepts of Risk Management 1

  1 The Essence of Risk Management 1

  2 Decision-making as the origin of risk management
     -Building up Risk Sensitivity 2

  3 The meanings of risk and risk management 3

  4 Risk Elements 4

  5 Concept of Risk Management and Crisis Management 6

  6 Risk Management in International Organization for Standardization 31000
     (ISO) 7

  7 Risk Management Process 7

     7.1 Establishing the context 7

     7.2 Risk Identification 8

     7.3 Risk Assessment 9

     7.4 Risk Treatments 10

  8 Three Cs in Risk Management (Choice, Communication and Coordination) ... 12

     8.1 Communication for common understanding of risk treatment 12

     8.2 Coordination for building a risk management system 13

  9 Dilemma of Decision-making 15

  Column1：Classics on Risk Management 16

  Column2：Three categories of risk by Kaplan and Mikes 16

Chapter 2   Crisis Management and Leadership

Case 1.   Tylenol Crisis and Response of Top Management
Johnson & Johnson (U.S.A.) 17

Introduction 17

1 Crisis that Rocked Confidence in the Company's Leading Product 17

2 Fulfilling Social Responsibility based upon its Corporate Philosophy 18

3 Denial of Unfavorable Fact Ruins Company 20

4 Recurrence of the Incident and Attitude of Dialogue Shown by the Top
Management 20

5 Decision of Chairman Burge who Apologized in a Live Broadcast 21

Chapter 3   Business Succession and Risk Management

Case 2.   Business Succession of "*Shinise*"-firms in Japan, which are
Referred to as Shops of Old Standing (Japan) 23

Introduction 23

1 Risk of business closure due to the dearth of successors 24

2 "Enterprise in existence for three hundred years";
"*Hitori ichigyo*", which is referred to as "one person for one business" and not
persisting in "primogeniture" 25

3 Entrepreneurs in Osaka to learn the essence of business succession and risk
management 27

Column3：Why are there so many 100-year-old firms in Japan? 28

Chapter 4   Health Management and Risk Management

Case 3.   Company's Approach Centered on "Health Training Hall"
Sunstar Inc. (Japan) 29

Introduction 29

1 Avoid Risk of Health of its Employees as a Company 29

2 Accommodation-type Guidance in Order to Regain Health Balance 30

3 Advocate Risk Management by Oral Care 31

Contents   v

Chapter 5   Natural Disasters and Risk Management (1)
Crisis Management and Leadership in March 11.

Case 4.   Leadership shown at "TEDxTohoku" (Japan) 33

Introduction 33

1 Great East Japan Earthquake and TEDxTohoku 33

2 Hideko Oikawa, Oikawa Denim 34

3 Kazuie Iinuma, Ishinomaki Red Cross Hospital 35

Chapter 6   Natural Disasters and Risk Management (2)

**Case 5.   Kumamoto Earthquakes and the Business Continuity Planning
(BCP) (Japan)** 37

Introduction 37

1 The 2016 Kyushu-Kumamoto Earthquakes 37

2 Success with BCP established as a lesson of earthquake disasters: Renesas
Electronics Corporation 38

3 Plans to reconsider BCP and practice drills for future operation after
suffering damages to production plants during the Kumamoto Earthquakes:
Sony Corporation 39

4 Quicker recovery than Kyushu Electric Power, utilizing generator vehicles
inside and outside the company: Tokyo Ohka Kogyo Co., Ltd. 40

Column4：Top Management Risk, most difficult internal risk to prevent 42

Chapter 7   Risk Taking: "Avoid" or "Retain"

Case 6.   Renault Espace (France) 43

Introduction 43

1 Renault's decision to launch the joint development of a new car and the result
of risk taking 43

2 Monopolized the minivan market in Europe 44

3 Matra had to shut-down despite its strategic success 44

4 Speculative risks should be taken after sufficient investigation / estimation 45

**Chapter 8　Safety and Risk Management in Sports Events
　　　　　　- Case of Citizen Marathons in Japan -**

Case 7.　Japanese Citizens' Marathon 47

Introduction 47

1 Review on Safety and Risk Management of Marathons 48

2 Case Study (1) : Isumi Kenkoh Marathon 49

3 Case Study (2) : Safety Management of the Marathon Race at Osaka

　Marathon 51

4 Case Study (3) : Kashiwa no ha marathon 51

5 Case Study (4) : Anti-terrorism measures and disaster management

　at the Tokyo Marathon 52

　5.1 Anti-terrorism 52

　5.2 Countermeasures for earthquakes 53

6 Risk Management Customized for Individual Needs and Respect to

　People in the Work Sites of Safety Management 54

Chapter 9　Interview 59

1 A Decision to retreat, and the courage to go forward
　Advance Create Co., Ltd. President/Founder, Yoshiharu Hamada 59

2 Enthusiasm for business is the key to risk management
　Ivresse Co., Ltd. Chief Executive Officer, Keiko Yamakawa 60

Column5：Business Succession in Wine Industry 63

Conclusion 65

Index 67

Chapter 1
Basic Concepts of Risk Management

1 The Essence of Risk Management

Books regarding risk management were published for the first time in the field of business administration in Japan in 1978. One of the two books was "Risk Management; New Growth Strategy in the Age of Crisis Pervasion" written by Zenji Katagata (President Inc., January 1978), which declared that risk management was for an enterprise to deal aggressively and proactively with uncertainty.

The other book, "Periphery of Crisis and Safety; Risk Management and Business Management" written by Toshiaki Kamei (Dohosha Printing, April 1978) advocated for a theory, which led to the present theory of Enterprise Risk Management (ERM).[1]

• The fundamental concept of risk management is to pay a fixed, small expense in the present, instead of an uncertain and larger cost in the future, which meant the concept of exchange

• Risk management is the scientific management against enterprise crises to avoid bankruptcy of the enterprise and to maintain reasonable business administration.

• Risk management departments must be assigned not as a line operational department, but as the staff department, which is in charge of both the general management staff and the functional management staff.

• Risk management's object is to survive in the age of crises pervasion, which requires management to cover overall risks of all kinds for the enterprise. The author, Toshiaki Kamei promoted the significance of a new type of risk management, which included "speculative risk" management, both in business management and business strategy, while the main stream at that time was the American theory of insurance management focusing only on "pure risk."

Further, Toshiaki Kamei published the first book in the field of enterprise risk management theory in Japan, "The Theory and Practice of Risk Management" (Diamond, Inc., 1980). He defined "risk management" in this book as follows:

• Risk management was an activity relying on risk prediction as a human instinct, to control and prepare risks, which could be an intentional interaction with uncertainty, as a rational transfer from risk to expenses, converting potential crises damage to expenses.

The essence of the theory in this book is still valid as a "classic" serving as a standard, or a guide to survive through the ages.

Risk management in business management is characterized as the following decision process: *Tokutei*, Identification (finding, recognizing and describing) → *Sohtei*, Estimation on probability and impact (analysis and evaluation) → *Kettei*, Decision (to determine a countermeasure); the three "*tei*"s. Furthermore, risk management is to exchange the possibility of a potential and uncertain accident in the future, for a practical and fixed small cost in the present; the examination of the risk balance of cost and benefit.

ISO 31000 (2009, 2018), International Organization for Standardization 31000, which is described in detail later, provided definitions of risk and risk management. According to ISO 31000, risk is "**an effect of uncertainty on objectives**" and risk management is "**a coordinated set of activities that are used to direct an organization and to control the risks.**"

The White Paper on Small and Medium Enterprises 2016 spent a whole chapter on risk management. The title of the fourth chapter was "Risk management to support money-making skills," which plainly revealed the nature of the present business risk management focusing on the desire for business value improvement.

2 Decision-making as the origin of risk management -Building up Risk Sensitivity

Peter L. Bernstein pointed out in his book titled "*Risk*," that the word "risk" derives from the early Italian "risicare," which means 'to dare.' This word had the meaning of trying with courage or wandering around a Rocky Mountain. In Bernstein's definition, risk is a choice or decision rather than a fate.[2]

These essential principles of risk theory suggest the important role of a leader for choice and decision making in managing risks, which requires a sensitivity to possible risks. The ability to notice a risk during a normal period, an intuitive sense, leadership, and the ability to communicate during an emergency are needed to make swift decisions.

Effective learning methods to build discipline in risk sensitivity are not only

Table 1.1

1) **Interaction with people who are different in fields, positions or ages**
2) **Experience with different cultures**
3) **Appreciation of art**
4) **Leaning from history; how decisions were made in confronting risks by historical people or well-known corporate managers**

used to devote themselves to their own specialty fields, but also to train in the following methods: shown in Table 1.1

3 The meanings of risk and risk management

In the study of risk management in the business field, risks have been classified into two categories, pure risk and speculative risk. Pure risk is a category of risk in which loss is the only possible negative outcome, such as accidents and disasters.

Table 1.2 Pure Risk and Speculative Risk

■ **Pure Risk ← Risk treatment (to respond to risks)**
- Loss Only Risk
- Risks that only produce negative effects (loss)
- Operational risk
- Accidents, disasters, liability
- Objects for which a decision is made to protect, avoid or insure

■ **Speculative Risk ← risk taking (to take a risk)**
- Loss or Gain Risk
- Possibility of negative effects(loss) and positive effects(gain)
- Business risk, strategic risk
- Start-up a new business, capital investment, fund procurement, mergers and acquisitions, which involve uncertainty of success or failure
- Objects for which a decision is made to take a business chance or a management strategy

Table 1.3 Relation of pure risk and speculative risk

Function	Risk			
	Speculative Risk	→	Pure Risk	
			Event	Result
Personnel	Employment and training of engineers for a new product development	→	Accidental death of an engineer after the training period	Loss of employment and training expenses
Production	Movement of a workshop for the improvement of productivity	→	Occurrence of a fire in a moved workshop	Loss of expenses related to movement
Sales	Cultivation of overseas sales market	→	Danger to customers due to product defect	Loss in investment

Jacques Charbonnier, *Le risk management*, L'Argus, 2007, p.33)

On the other hand, speculative risk is a category of risk that is an uncertain risk accompanied by a business chance and will either result in a loss or gain.

These days social risk has been a serious problem, such as natural catastrophes and novel influenza, which has a great impact on the whole society. Thus, the view point of social risk management as a countermeasure is remarkably important. The point is that social risk management is not an endeavor for the survival of an individual company seeking short-term interest, but for cooperative activity, where an enterprise must bear the risk management with individuals, households, schools and public administrations in the community.

Furthermore, in this present society, risk management has been facing the problem of mental health, which more and more people have been complaining about. A preparation and provision system for risk management is imperative for humans themselves and their minds, as well as funds and assets.

4 Risk Elements

Risk management started as insurance management and safety management. In the year 2002, the International Organization for Standardization (ISO) 73, "Risk Management -Vocabulary- Guidelines for use in standards"was published and defined risk as a combination of the consequences of an event and the associated likelihood of occurrence. In the concept of traditional risk management of pure risk, risk was regarded as "a possibility of accident occurrence." As shown in Figure1.1, it covers such elements as (1)hazard, circumstances and conditions that affect accident occurrence, (2)exposure, people and objects that are exposed to risk, (3)risk, possibility of accident occurrence, (4)peril, accident or disaster, (5) crisis, nearing of accident breakout and persistence of accident occurrence, and (6) loss. It is effective to clarify which of these elements to approach in applying risk management.[3]

Basic Concepts of Risk Management

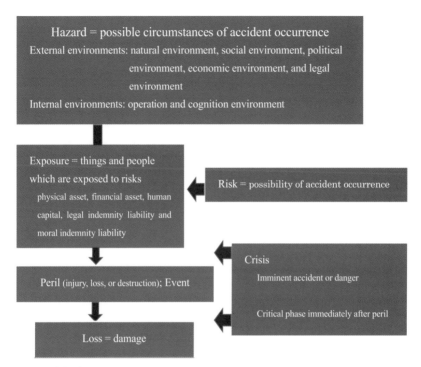

Fig. 1.1 Risk Elements

Table 1.4 Hazard (Condition and circumstance that could affect accident-generation) and examples of basic risk response

Hazard 1	Disorganized equipment and storage facility Lack of maintenance	Risk response	Regulation of cleaning and maintenance procedures
Hazard 2	Flood	Risk response	Management of water source
Hazard 3	Waste water treatment	Risk response	Appropriate maintenance of the water treatment facility
Hazard 4	Deteriorated and frozen surface of a parking lot	Risk response	Snow removal and sprinkling road anti-icing agent Periodic maintenance

(Peter C. Young and Steven C. Tippins, *Managing Business Risk*, AMACOM, 2000, p.143)

Table 1.5 Peril (Accidents that cause loss) and examples of basic risk response

Peril 1	Fire	Risk response	Utilization of fireproof building materials
Peril 2	Earthquake	Risk response	Renovation of the building
Peril 3	Dearth of lighting in the parking lot	Risk response	Installation of additional lighting and enhancement of security
Peril 4	Slippery staircases in a retail store	Risk response	Utilization of non skid materials

(Peter C. Young and Steven C. Tippins, *Managing Business Risk*, AMACOM, 2000, p.143)

5　Concept of Risk Management and Crisis Management

The relation between risk management and crisis management is summarized as follows:

The word "crisis" means the "turning point" of whether the situation worsens. We can map crises into four stages of illness, "prodromal crisis stage," "acute crisis stage," "chronic crisis stage," and "crisis resolution stage". Fink defined "Crisis management – planning for a crisis, a turning point – is the art of removing much of the risk and uncertainty to allow you to achieve more control over your own destiny."[4]

Table 1.6

■ **In advance; Risk Management**
- Exertion of "Risk Sensitivity" as an ability of recognition
- Identification and assessment of risks, to find or reveal
- Risk treatment; Disaster countermeasures, Prevention of accidents, Insurance and Preparation of fund reserve
- Safety Management Plan and Business Continuity Plan (BCP)
- Simulation training; risk-conscious training in a normal period
- Common understanding and system formulation regarding what risk to identify and how to respond to risks

■ **After the fact; Crisis Management**
- Exertion of "Risk Sensitivity" as an ability of decision-making
- Leadership, decisions and communication
- Determinate message of the leader; what is happening and what direction to go
- Resilience
- After a time lapse; learning through a failure or a disaster as a lesson

Basic Concepts of Risk Management

6 Risk Management in International Organization for Standardization 31000 (ISO)

International Organization for Standardization 31000, "Risk management -Principles and guideline" was published in 2009 to provide guidance as an international standard for how to develop risk management. According to this guideline, the risk management standard in Japan was revised from JIS Q 2001 of "Guidelines for development and implementation of risk management systems" to JIS Q 31000 as the Japanese translation ver. of ISO 31000.

Although there are diversified views in the risk management field, we think that the ISO framework must be respected, which was created by experts in varied fields of study. For example, the framework of the risk management process shown in ISO 31000 could be a criterion of risk management for implementation into all kinds of organizations, including large corporations.

ISO 31000 was revised in February 2018. The Japanese translation of ISO3100:2018 is now JIS Q 31000:2019.

7 Risk Management Process

Fig. 1.2. shows the risk management process in ISO 31000: 2009. The processes of risk management takes the form of (1)communication and consultation and (2)monitoring and review interacting with each other at each stage of (a)establishing the context, (b)risk assessment(identification, analysis and evaluation) or (c)risk treatment.

ISO 31000 was revised in 2018. ISO 31000: 2018 replaced "establishing the context" with "Scope, context and criteria" and added "Recording and Reporting" at the end of the process.

7.1 Establishing the context

ISO 31000:2009 shows that the first step in the risk management process is "Establishing the context." For the most appropriate risk management to be developed for an individual organization, establishing the context is required. Three points for establishing context are as follows:

i.   The current condition and circumstance you are in.
ii. Your available resources.
iii. The principles you hold and the strategies you develop.

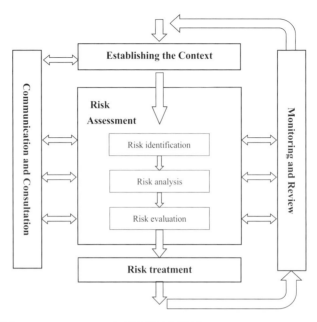

Fig. 1.2 Risk management process in ISO 31000: 2009

ISO 31000:2018 replaced "establishing the context" with "Scope, context and criteria"

7.2 Risk Identification

According to ISO 31000:2009, after establishing the context, risk assessment is conducted. The first step of risk assessment is risk identification, which involves finding, recognizing and describing the risks. The following are examination points:
  i. What human resources and physical resources the organization has; the review of human capital and physical capital and the analysis of risk exposure
  ii. What accident could occur; human risk and physical risk
  What accident could be induced; responsibility risk and expense risk
  iii. What forms accidents could occur in; human loss, physical loss, uncollectible debt, loss of concession and compensation liability
  Risk identification employs the various following methods:
  i. Field validation
  ii. Hearing investigation

iii. Check list

iv. Flow chart

Furthermore, Heinrich's law must be taken into consideration in risk identification. There are incidents which are called "*hiyari*, *hatto* incidents"; *hiyari* and *hatto* are Japanese expressions uttered at the moment when feeling a slight danger and often results in the person being startled and making a sudden motion, which can be a factor in the cause of accidents. The Heinrich Pyramid shows that when these "*hiyari*, *hatto*" occupational accidents occur, a common ratio of the seriousness of injuries is: for each three-hundred potential "*hiyari*, *hatto*" incidents, twenty-nine people will be injured, and one person will have a fatal or near-fatal injury. Experiencing these moments could be a bifurcation to either a success or a failure in risk management; being attentive with the consciousness of the possibility of a disaster or just passing through with relief of not leading to a disaster.

In risk identification, three risk patterns must be observed as follows:

Table 1.7 Three aspects of risk

• Risk hides.
• Risk changes.
• Risk repeats.

7.3 Risk Assessment

The objectives of risk assessments are to analyze and evaluate the identified risks and to estimate the level of impact and the consequences of the risks. What should be assessed is as follows:

i. Probability and frequency of accidents

ii. Scale of the loss induced by the accident, that is, the severity of the accident

Identified risks must be examined. It is assessed how probable and frequently an accident could occur in reality and, as a result, how and the enormity of the accident could impact the result.

This risk assessment is shared as a risk map throughout the organization. The purpose of risk mapping is to visualize the identified and assessed risk. In order to improve risk management for the overall organization, not only personnel who are in charge of risk management, but all members must have a full understanding of the risks. Therefore, the risk map is created to increase visibility of risks so that anyone could easily recognize risk management. A risk matrix chart is generally used to define the severity and frequency of the risk. It has been recognized that preparation and response to low-probability but high-consequence risks are required, especially since the 2011 East Japan Earthquake. Extreme events including major natural disasters occur at a small frequency but if they occur once, huge damages are caused at a severe scale.

Eisai Co., Ltd. has been operating Control Self-Assessment (CSA), with a Compliance Risk Management Promotion Division working in the center to cooperate with unit chiefs for ten years. Concretely, nine-hundred chiefs are given a task to extract five risks and to suggest their countermeasures. Consequently, three thousand and five hundred risks are listed, which are assessed from the viewpoint of impact and are categorized. Six months later, the effects of the countermeasures are examined.

7.4 Risk Treatments

Risk treatment comprises two props and four measures as shown in Table 1.8. The two props are "risk control" (prevention of accidents and disaster countermeasures) and "risk finance" (preparation of fund reserve and application of insurance). Four measures are "avoidance," "removal and mitigation" "imputation, transference and sharing" and "retention and acceptance".

Taking an example of driving a car under the conditions of poor physical health or sleep deprivation, risk treatments are explained as follows:
■ Risk Control
• Avoidance of a risk; to stop driving a car until conditions improve
• Elimination or reduction of a risk=prevention of an accident in advance; to slow down the speed in driving or to drive attentively on the left and the right and also in the front and the back
• Reducing a loss after an accident; to fasten a seat belt
■ Risk Finance
• Transferring a risk; to obtain insurance

In the case of taking an action without avoiding a risk, we try to reduce or mitigate as much of the risk as possible. Still, risk remains, which is referred to as residual risk. The transfer of a residual risk to others is attempted so the risk can be shared with others. If there still remains risk which cannot be reduced, transferred or shared. That risk must be retained.

Retention of a risk is classified into two groups as follows:
  • Passive retention; risk retention due to the ignorance of a risk
  • Active retention; risk retention with full recognition of the risk

Precisely, even if a risk is recognized, active retention is classified into two groups. One is postponed risk, where the recognized risk is left without any countermeasures. The other active retention of a risk is to actively or positively retain the risk, having full understanding the existence of the risk, which is totally

Basic Concepts of Risk Management 11

different from the condition where an organization is exposed or confronted with a risk without knowing that they have had a risk. ISO 31000 also recommends this active retention of risk as the condition where risks are retained by decision-making based on the information.

Risk management strategy to make the decision of retaining a risk could be "partial retention" and "safety valve". The decision must be made while considering how to treat the risk, and whether to retain either all or part of a risk. Risk is completely retained. Partial risk is retained after avoiding, reducing or transferring some part. Decision-making also requires the consideration of a "safety valve" to transfer a risk to.

ISO31000:2009 and ISO 31000: 2018 define risk treatment as a process with the following:

- Avoiding the risk by deciding not to start or continue the activity that gives rise to the risks
- Taking or increasing the risk in order to pursue an opportunity
- Removing the risk resource
- Changing the likelihood
- Changing the consequences
- Sharing the risk (e.g. through contracts, buying insurance)
- Retaining the risk by informed decision[5]

Table 1.8 Risk Control and Risk Finance

Risk Control	
Hard Control: Physical prevention in advance, prevention of an accident, and introduction of a damage reduction countermeasure Soft Control: Shared values, common understanding, education and training	
Avoidance	Discontinuance of an action accompanied by risk
Removal (elimination) and mitigation (reduction)	Prevention of a risk (prevention and mitigation) and dispersion and integration of risk
Risk Finance Financial measures prepared for an accident occurrence, financing and compensation after an accident occurrence, and raising funds	
Transferring (to an external agency) Sharing (joint owning)	Utilization of insurance, mutual aid and money fund, and Alternative Risk Transfer (ART)
Retention and Acceptance	Risk burden, self-insurance and captive

Ueda shows 8 key concepts of process to build up corporate resilience and sustainability in risk management as the followings:[6]

(1) Learn from past failures
(2) Assess your own potential future risks and think flexibly
(3) Detect changes in risk and respond
(4) Develop corporative vision
(5) Incorporate culture vision into the business and formulate risk management process
(6) Visualize and balance risks and opportunities
(7) Share values with stakeholders, especially employees
(8) Build up resilience by accepting reality, sustaining the vision and thinking flexibly

8 Three Cs in Risk Management (Choice, Communication and Coordination)

Risk management is, before everything else, decision-making regarding Choice of risk treatment. This decision is supported by Communication and Coordination.

8.1 Communication for common understanding of risk treatment

Fig.1.3 shows risk communication in a business administration means to build common understanding of both (a) members inside an organization and (b) its

Risk communication inside an organization

(a) Communication inside an organization Top management ⟷ Middle management ⟷ Worksite	(b) Communication between an organization and its stakeholders outside the organization An organization ⟷ Its stakeholders: stockholders, investors, consumers and local community

↓　Disclosure of risk information

i. Common understanding of risks surrounding the organization →Shared values of the condition of risks

ii. Common understanding of risk responses →Shared values of overcoming risks

Fig. 1.3 Risk Communication

Basic Concepts of Risk Management 13

stakeholders outside the organization in regard to the following:
  i. What risk the organization is confronted with
  ii. How the organization will respond to the risk

Examples for this are "announcement" in a general meeting of stockholders, the following information included in the Annual Securities Report: "Challenges to be addressed," "business risks," "analysis of financial position, operating results, and cash flows" and "the condition of corporate governance," and also the information related to internal control of "regulation of the loss risk management and the other risk of internal control management systems."

Eisai Co., Ltd., showed the following "risk factors associated with the company": risks related to safety and quality issues of products, possible incidence of adverse events, risks related to lawsuits, risks related to compliance with laws and regulations, risks related to intellectual property, uncertainties in new drug development, risks related to medical fee restriction measures, risks related to generic products, risks related to challenges arising out of global expansion, risks related to strategic alliances with partners, risks related to corporate acquisition and product acquisition, outsourcing-related risks, risks related to IT security and information management, risks related to internal control management system in financial reports, foreign exchange fluctuations, risks related to the closure or shutdown of factories, risks related to the environment and risks related to natural disasters.

8.2   Coordination for building a risk management system

ISO 31000 (2009, 2018) defined Risk Management as "a coordinated set of activities that is used to direct an organization and to control the risks."

A risk committee system has been established in an enterprise to be in charge of coordination for risk management. Although risks of production, sales and information, which are related to individual functional sections, are managed by the section respectively, risks covering multiple sections and risks affecting the organization overall must be treated by the risk management committee.

Eisai Co., Ltd. thoroughly implemented Enterprise Resource Management (ERM) in 2016. The Risk Management Committee consists of five members including two executives, which is responsible for cross-departmental and company-wide risks. The director of Compliance and the Risk Management Department is assigned as the chairperson of the committee.

Concerning the organization of risk management, Crockford explains as follows:

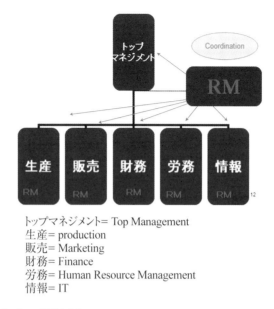

トップマネジメント= Top Management
生産= production
販売= Marketing
財務= Finance
労務= Human Resource Management
情報= IT

Fig. 1.4 Organization of Risk Management

The way in which risk management is organized must be in keeping with the company style. If the company is decentralized, then risk management must also be decentralized. A central risk management department seeking to influence the way in which day-to-day risk management should be carried on is unlikely to have any success. Much more probably, it would be seen as an interfering arm of central management, to be viewed with extreme suspicion and given as little co-operation as possible. In such a company, it will probably be more effective to establish a number of separate decentralized risk management advisory functions. A central risk manager will still be needed, but his function may very well be that of a co-ordinator of co-ordinators.[7]

Whatever risk management system may be constructed, it is required that both managers and workers should have a shared value to develop their sensitivity.

Basic Concepts of Risk Management

9 Dilemma of Decision-making

Unfortunately, it is impossible to be in s state where there is no risk. However, as *"Risuku is Kusuri,"* *"Risk is Medicine"* says "Risk could make us grow." When "Risk" threatens an enterprise, they make efforts to overcome the risk. Therefore, the enterprise can progress and improve its value.

Note:

1) COSO, *Enterprise Risk Management – Integrating with Strategy and Performance,* June 2017.
2) Peter L. Bernstein, *Against the Gods,* "*Risuku:Kamigami heno Hangyaku*" Translated by *Mamoru Aoyama, Nihonkeizai shinnbun sha,* Nikkei Inc., 1998, p.23.
3) Perter C. Young and Steven C. Tippins, *Managing Business Risk,* AMACOM, 2000, PP.65-101. ("*MBA no risuku manejimento*" Translated by *Miyakawa, Takahashi and Sakamoto, PHP kenkyujo,* PHP Institute, 2002, p. 262); Yoshinari Hayashi and Katsuyuki Kamei, "Risk Management", Seiji Abe, Mamoru Ozawa, Yoshiaki Kawata ed., *Science of Societal Safety Living at Times of Risks and Disasters,* Springer, 2018, Chapter 11, p.124.
4) Steven Fink, *Crisis Management: Planning for the inevitable,* American Management Association, 1986, p.15.
5) *ISO 31000:2018 (JIS Q31000:2019),* Mutual translation, pocket version, Nihon Kikaku Kyokai, 2019, pp.88-90.
6) Kazuo Ueda, "Common factors of Corporate Resilience and Implications for Social Enterprise –Resilience Thinking and Japanese Case Studies –" Bulletin of the Research Institute of Commerce, Vol.46 No.3, July 2014, p.16
7) Neil Crockford, *An Introduction to Risk Management,* Woodhead-Faulkner, 1980, pp.102-103.

Exercise:

What is your definition of risk management?

Column 1: Classics on Risk Management

<Security Function in Business Administration>
Henri Fayol, *Administration industrielle et générale*, 1916
<Cost of Risk Management>
Russell B. Gallagher, "Risk Management: New Phase of Cost Control" *Harvard Business Review*, September/October 1956, pp.75-86.
<Business Risk Management>
Robert I. Mehr and Bob A. Hedges, *Risk Management in the Business Enterprise*, Irwin, 1963.
<Insurance based theory of Risk Management>
C. Arthur Williams, Jr. and Richard M. Heins, *Risk Management and Insurance*, McGraw-Hill, 1964.
<Pioneer in France>
Jacques Charbonnier, *La Gestion de la Sécurité de l'Entreprise*, L'Argus, 1976.
(Jacques Charbonnier, Lexique du RISK MANAGEMENT, afnor, 2019. =His last work)
<Pioneer in Great Britain>
Neil Crockford, *An Introduction to Risk Management*, Woodhead-Faulkner, 1980,
<Crisis Management>
Steven Fink, *Crisis Management Planning for the Inevitable*, Amacom, 1986.

Column 2: Three categories of risk by Kaplan and Mikes

Kaplan and Mikes (2012) show that risks fall into one of three categories.

Category I : **Preventable risks** (arising from unauthorized, illegal, unethical, incorrect, or inappropriate actions)
Category II : **Strategy risk** (voluntarily accepted in order to generate superior returns from strategy)
Category III : **External risk** (such as natural and political disasters and major macroeconomic shifts)

(Robert S. Kaplan and Anette Mikes, "Managing Risks: A New Framework", Harvard *Business Review*, June 2012 issue.
https://hbr.org/2012/06/managing-risks-a-new-framework)

Chapter 2
Crisis Management and Leadership

Case 1. Tylenol Crisis and Response of Top Management Johnson & Johnson (U.S.A.)

Introduction

When a company faces a crisis, it is important that top management accepts facts, without denying unfavorable facts, and makes the best use of communication resources. This company was successful in crisis management by responding to a crisis by devoting itself to its "management philosophy," and eventually, they could protect the company's brand as well as their employees.

Owing to economic globalization and the remarkable development of infrastructure in information and communication, enterprises are exposed to daily changes in business environment. When we establish and develop an enterprise, it is quite natural that we assume risks that may happen during that process. However, recently, it is not an uncommon situation that we face a crisis that nobody could envision. How does the top management leading the business overcome difficult situations? What kinds of leadership actions do they take?

1 Crisis that Rocked Confidence in the Company's Leading Product

Johnson and Johnson[1] is a global health-care company. Today, it covers a diverse business area of adhesive plaster, mouth wash, cosmetics, contact lens, etc. for general consumers. When it was founded, it was producing and selling medical supplies such as the world first sterile bandage and emergency bandage "band aid." It placed an emphasis on health care, and it has not changed in that respect. It was the Tylenol crisis that rocked its confidence in this field. Tylenol was the biggest-selling painkiller in the United States at that time, a leading product of the company, and approximately one hundred thousand Americans were taking it (it is still on sale now). It can be easily imagined that if its sale was discontinued, it would have affected the management of the company.

In September 29, 1982, a 12-year-old girl died an unexplained death in the city of Chicago, Illinois, followed by the deaths of seven people, and it was rumored that the "Tylenol painkiller" was found at each site of the incident. Local media inquired at Johnson and Johnson about the relationship of these cases to the product.

A public affairs manager immediately reported the incident occurrences and the rumor among the mass media to Burge, the chairman and CEO. A board meeting was convened the day following the incident. Furthermore, 90 minutes after that, the public affair manager, the vice president of Johnson and Johnson, and David Collins, chairman of McNeil Consumer Product (hereafter referred as to McNeil), an affiliated firm of Johnson and Johnson producing Tylenol, rushed to McNeil's Fort Washington plant in the state of Pennsylvania by helicopter and investigated the manufacturing site.

The result of the investigation showed that a perpetrator mixed a cyanogens compound into Tylenol, and this was the cause of death. There was no problem with Tylenol. However, Chairman Burge appeared himself on prime time news and called for consumers to stop taking Tylenol and to stop selling it to pharmacies and medical workers. He also declared that the company would develop a drug container to prevent foreign objects being mixed in and the old container would be replaced with a new model.

2 Fulfilling Social Responsibility based upon its Corporate Philosophy

The company has a corporate philosophy called "Our Credo." (Fig. 2.1.)

Excerpts from "Our Credo" of Johnson and Johnson[2]

The first responsibility is for doctors, nurses, patients and all consumers including parents who are using our products and services.

The second responsibility is for all their employees and everyone working in the world.

The third responsibility is to the community where we are living and working, and furthermore to be collaborative with all societies in the world.

The fourth responsibility is to the shareholders.

Crisis Management and Leadership   19

Our Credo

We believe our first responsibility is to the doctors, nurses and patients, to mothers and
fathers and all others who use our products and services. In meeting their needs everything
we do must be of high quality. We must constantly strive to reduce our costs in order to
maintain reasonable prices. Customers' orders must be serviced promptly and accurately.
Our suppliers and distributors must have an opportunity to make a fair profit.

We are responsible to our employees, the men and women who work with us throughout
the world. Everyone must be considered as an individual. We must respect their dignity
and recognize their merit. They must have a sense of security in their jobs. Compensation
must be fair and adequate, and working conditions clean, orderly and safe. We must be
mindful of ways to help our employees fulfill their family responsibilities. Employees
must feel free to make suggestions and complaints. There must be equal opportunity
for employment, development and advancement for those qualified. We must provide
competent management, and their actions must be just and ethical.

We are responsible to the communities in which we live and work and to the world
community as well. We must be good citizens – support good works and charities and
bear our fair share of taxes. We must encourage civic improvements and better health
and education. We must maintain in good order the property we are privileged to use,
protecting the environment and natural resources.

Our final responsibility is to our stockholders. Business must make a sound profit. We must
experiment with new ideas. Research must be carried on, innovative programs developed
and mistakes paid for. New equipment must be purchased, new facilities provided and
new products launched. Reserves must be created to provide for adverse times. When we
operate according to these principles, the stockholders should realize a fair return.

Johnson & Johnson

---

https://www.jnj.com/credo/

Fig. 2.1 Our Credo by Johnson & Johnson

If this case is objectively looked at, McNeil producing Tylenol and Johnson and
Johnson had no relation to the perpetrator, or rather they were victims who were
involved in the incident. They could have had the option to stick to the attitude that
"Our company is the victim."

However, the company placed the priority on fulfilling its responsibility to those
specified in "Our Credo," or in other words, accepting its social responsibility.
Although there was no manual for this purpose, it had clearly stated the company's
philosophy to take a consistent attitude as a company toward any situation it faces.
It can be said that it is a source of great success in risk management.

It stopped the sales of its products so that there would be no more victims,
and stuck to a strategy of transparent communication so that every person,
including consumers and employees, feel relieved even if only slightly. More

specifically, positive dispatch of information such as the installation of toll-free phone lines for inquiries from consumers, a full-page advertisement and spot commercial on national major papers, more than 2,000 questionnaire phone calls, coverage by several hundred hours of radio and TV reports, financial backing for McNeil, employment support for laid-off employees and so on and so forth. It is said in America that this case had been the most often reported in the media since the Vietnam War. In addition to these external communications, internal communications also were emphasized.

The incident resulted in the loss of seven lives, thirty-one million capsules were retrieved, and the incident cost more than $100 million. It is better that no such crisis occurs. However, once it has occurred, the company accepted and responded to it, and eventually, consumers evaluated their response to the crisis and among other things, employees deepened ties with each other and they became proud of their company[3].

3 Denial of Unfavorable Fact Ruins Company

Professor Richard S. Tedlow[4] referred to the Tylenol Crisis in his book titled "Why Business Leaders Fail to Look Facts in the Face," and said that it is a failure of risk management that when a company faces a crisis, the top management "denies the facts unfavorable to them" and it causes the failure of their risk management and the ruin of the company. Today, there are many companies that manualized specific terms such as the flow and focus of responsibility which are to be announced during an emergency. However, before that time, top management should understand the following lessons.

4 Recurrence of the Incident and Attitude of Dialogue Shown by the Top Management

The second incident

Unfortunately, a similar incident occurred. On February 7, 1986, four years after the first incident, a 23-year-old woman suddenly died in Yonkers, in the state of New York. The female victim took two capsules of Tylenol 12 hours prior to her death. The results of the autopsy showed that death was caused by a cyanogens compound, so that it was easily supposed that a case of contamination of foreign matter occurred, the same as in the previous case.

Johnson & Johnson determined (1) to indefinitely stop TV CM broadcasting of all Tylenol products, (2) and that Burge, CEO, would have a press conference. The press conference was held on February 11, four days after the incident.

In this press conference, it was stated that because the region where this incident occurred was limited, unlike the previous case, the company would not carry out a nationwide recall[5]. In the third press conference held on February 17, it was announced that it had stopped the production of Tylenol capsules and promoted switching to Tylenol caplets (capsule-shaped pill) as a substitute for consumers. He said "It would cost 150 million dollars, but it cannot be compared with the grief of the victim, her bereaved family and friends".

5 Decision of Chairman Burge who Apologized in a Live Broadcast

What is noteworthy here is the interview that Chairman Burge received in the news program in a live broadcast the day following the news conference. During the program, an MC conveyed what the mother of dead woman said "The decision of Johnson and Johnson was three years late. If it had decided to discontinue the production of Tylenol capsule when the incident occurred four years ago, my daughter would not have had to die."

Listening to this, Chairman Burge said "If I were the mother of the victim, I would have said the same thing (what the mother said) and I would have had the same feeling. Repentance always comes too late. I think I should not have put the Tylenol capsule on the market again at that time"6). For this, Professor Tedlow described in his book as follows: "In a litigation society like America, Burge admitted the fault of the company that he was leading during a live broadcast. There was acceptance of reality, which is an extreme opposite of rejection. Burge recognized that what he faces is human emotion. In the society where public figures say something different from reality and tell lies without hesitation, Burge did not deny facts unfavorable to them and spoke only the truth. As a result, he was able to protect the brand of his company[7].

Although Professor Tedlow describes the event above, the deed of top management accepting realty and apologizing raises the risk of the litigation to the company, so it does not always lead to positive results from the perspective of risk management. That is why the top management carefully chooses their words in an interview and others often disavow what they could. Even when they apologize, they describe in what part of the case they admit their fault in detail and apologize.

However, Professor Tedlow points out in his book that those in the top

22   Chapter 2

management positions do not disavow their responsibility "because they do not face reality, but not because they misjudge the reality" and as a result, they become unable to avoid failure that they otherwise could[8]. This attitude may partly overlap with that of Chairman Burge. His decision to accept reality and apologize led to sincerity and built up a new relationship of trust.

When the top management is exposed to a crisis, how to make a judgment depends upon the situation, and it is very difficult for them. If we stand in the position of top management, it is best for risk management to presume the worst-case scenario and simulate their response to that situation. Let's ask ourselves what we would do, not as the response of top management but as individuals.

Note:

1) Johnson & Johnson was founded in New Brunswick, New Jersey, 1886 by three brothers of Robert Wood Johnson, James Wood Johnson and Edward Mead Johnson. It is known for the development of medical and healthcare related products including the world first innovative sterile surgical bandage. It is now the biggest general healthcare company in the world after mergers and acquisitions.
2) Jonson & Jonson, homepage https:/www.jnj.co.jp/group/credo/index.html (Our Credo)
3) Richard S. Tedlow - *Why Business Leaders Fail to Look Facts in the face - Eight lessons for facing reality*. Translated by Nami Hijikata, Published by Nikkei Publishing Inc., 2011.
4) Professor of Harvard Business School (Business Management). There is another book titled *Andy Grove*. translated by Hiroko Ariga, published by Diamond, Inc.
5) Recall means that when some defect was found in a product, in order to minimize the generation and expiation of the incidents, the manufactures and others of the products stop its distribution and sales, or exchange with other product, remake or take back the product.
6) Tedlaw, *ibid.*
7) *ibid.*
8) *ibid.*

Exercise:

How can corporate philosophy influence risk management in your organization?

Chapter 3
Business Succession and Risk Management

Case 2. Business Succession of *"Shinise"*-firms in Japan, which are Referred to as Shops of Old Standing (Japan)

Introduction

Decision-making is required for business management succession; whom, when and how to succeed. Successors must make a decision of how they would respect the business approaches of the predecessor, and at the same time, how they would develop new businesses with the promotion of individuality and originality. Needless to say, these decisions entail a grave risk of failure.

Japan has been leading the world in the longevity of firms in business for a century or more. However, problems related to business management succession are being exposed, which are social risks. Scenarios and problems of successions differ from one company to another. It would be rewarding for the goal of business succession to analyze information of business succession of various enterprises and to prepare succession planning from an early stage.

- Business succession is not intended to manage the business merely by following the business approach of the predecessor. The successor must regard the succession as a starting point for the growth of the business and have the courage to take risks for business opportunities, while being committed to succeeding with the core business skills.
- Prior preparation needs to be done. It is important to study diversified cases of business succession. The key to the accomplishment of business succession is to prepare in advance and have a clear vision for what an enterprise can and should do before and after the succession.

1 Risk of business closure due to the dearth of successors

According to the White Paper on Small and Medium Enterprises published in 2006, approximately 70,000 enterprises discontinued business in a year period due to the dearth of successors among the 290,000 enterprises which discontinued business. The scenario that small and medium enterprises had difficulties in finding successors for their businesses has been a serious problem, and a grave risk for socioeconomics. The number of companies, and the number of employees of small and medium enterprises (hereinafter referred to as "SMEs"), account for ninety percent and seventy percent respectively of all companies in Japan. SMEs have been playing a vital role in producing technologies and services as an innovative and creative pioneer, and have contributed to the dynamic Japanese economy in both quantitative and qualitative aspects. It is a grave risk that SMEs frequently fail at business succession, and even discontinue their business in the worst case, because they do not have a successor.

Major problems in succession of SME businesses are "finding the right successor," "how to sell business interest properly," "emotional gap between the predecessor and the successor" and "issues related to laws and taxes," which are easily induced as social risks. In addition to the risks of business succession, there are intertwined risks in the risk management of SMEs. Typical risks are as follows:

1) The family business or SMEs owners do not recognize the existence of the risk.
2) The managers are aware of the risk but take no countermeasures in advance.
3) Even when the risks are recognized and an ex post facto measure is taken in haste, it is too late to treat the risks properly; especially when the owner is faced with aging or deteriorating health and their retirement is imminent.
4) Complex problems related to the material issues of assets and funds and the mental issues of human relationships and emotion.

The most important factor in risk management is to plan early, where risk treatment must be scrutinized in five- to ten-year spans. It must be kept in mind that a makeshift or a temporary measure has no value or effect.

Risk management in business succession is intended to clarify the risk treatment process, identifying, visualizing risks and making a business succession plan describing how risk treatment must be conducted in each stage. Thus, smooth and effective succession can be secured. As for the material issue of assets and finances, the system of policies and laws can be utilized, and also advisors of financial institutions and tax counselors can support the succession process. However, it is not simple to take a measure in the aspect of the mental issues, such as human relationships and emotions[1].

Business Succession and Risk Management   25

2   "Enterprise in existence for three hundred years"; "*Hitori ichigyo*", which is referred to as "one person for one business" and not persisting in "primogeniture"

Although business succession has been a serious problem as a social issue in Japan, Japan is still leading the world in the longevity of enterprises. According to research data published by the Bank of Korea in 2008, while there were 5,586 enterprises with more than two hundred years of history in 44 countries in the world, Japanese enterprises accounted for more than fifty percent of that number, with 3,146 enterprises. Teikoku Databank, Ltd. showed, in research data published in 2013, that among 1,440,000 business entities in Japan, 26,144 business entities were established at least one hundred years ago.

Teikoku Databank also announced the number of enterprises by prefecture in terms of those established for one hundred years, and Kyoto prefecture earned the first rank. *Hori kinhakufun*, Hori Metal Leaf & Powder Co., Ltd. with a three hundred year history is introduced as an example here.

Hori Metal Leaf & Powder was established by Denbei Hori in 1711 (in the middle of the Edo Period) Over the generations, the company has made unremitting efforts and has succeeded. For example, the seventh president, Shintaro Hori started the new manufacture of various metal leaf powders in addition to the traditional business of gold foil manufacturing and processing[2]. During the world financial crisis and the Second World War, they developed a new kind of colored foil in order to survive the government control of gold production[3]. "*Shinwa haku*", the new foil, was a silver foil whose color looked golden due to colorizing. Through these processes, *Hori kinhakufun* established two family mottos. One family rule is "*Hitori Ichigyo*," which is referred to as "one person for one business." This policy means that no matter how many sons the predecessor had, only one son succeeds the family business and other sons were forbidden to run the same kind of business. The other family rule is to determine the correct successor through meritocracy. Not persisting in "primogeniture," they have been free to choose a successor with the criteria of the ability and resources to manage business[4]. The ninth president, Etsuaki Hori was recognized to have an excellent nature as a manager in his childhood and was brought up in a different way from his brothers. He lived under the same roof of the premises when he went to high school and university. Every morning he cleaned the firm and he also helped packing and sending products with employees. He even participated in business operation. Later on, he was still young when he succeeded the family business. However, there was no objection from any employees including *banto*, the head clerk and veterans, who had seen him working hard with them since he was a boy[5]. At present, Tomoyuki Hori serves as the tenth president. The spirit of *shinise* (a long-established business or a long standing company) with three centuries of history is the dogged determination to maintain the quality of the business. They would compete on value, not on price.

Furthermore, they adhere to the following company philosophy;
1) The harmony of the employees
2) Pursuit of a sound and long-lasting business with the appropriate size (not pursuing short-term interest or expansion of business)
3) Priority in trust; management policies are non-debt management and an equity ratio over eighty five percent.)
4) Tradition must be a sequence of innovations

Fig. 3.1 Hori Metal Leaf & Powder, Mr. and Mrs. Hori with professors from Witten Institute for Family Business (WIFU, Witten/Herdecke University)
(April 2019, photograph by Katsuyuki Kamei)

Business Succession and Risk Management 27

3 Entrepreneurs in Osaka to learn the essence of business succession and risk management

Studying examples of business succession and risk management in Japan, we learn from entrepreneurs associated with Osaka to examine entrepreneurship and its movement. Here case studies of enterprises and entrepreneurs were chosen from the Entrepreneurial museum of challenge and innovation[6] in Osaka, which was established by the Osaka Chamber of Commerce and Industry. Three approaches are introduced as follows:

1) Risk taking; to dare to take a risk for a challenge in a new field or a change of policy direction
2) Expansion and development of the business due to the business succession
3) Inheritance of the tradition and the excellent or exquisite skills to maintain their business as "*Shinise*" firms

Table 3.1 Three approaches to entrepreneurship

「リスクテーキングをした事例」
Multiple Cases of Risk-Taking
「事業継承により拡大・発展」
Expansion and Development due to the Business Succession
「伝統や優れた技術を継承してきた老舗」
Lasting "Shinise" Firms with Inheritance of Tradition and Excellent or Exquisite Skills

Note:

1) Katsuyuki Kamei, "*Gendai Risk Management no kisoriron to jirei*", Horitu Bunka Sha, 2014, p.156
2) Hori Metal Leaf & Powder, "Keieirinen no keisho-keieijinruigakusha no siten", *PHP Business Review*, PHP Research Institute, Inc., March and April 2010.
3) *ibid.*
4) *ibid.*
5) *ibid.*
6) The Entrepreneurial Museum of Challenge and Innovation. This museum was inaugurated by Osaka Chamber of Commerce and Industry in June 2001.

Exercise:

Choose one 'shinise' firm. What is a key factor of success for its survival?

Column 3: Why are there so many 100-year-old firms in Japan?

Explanations by Toshio GOTO, "Longevity of Japanese family firm" in Poutziouris et al., *Handbook of Research on Family Business*, Edward Elgar Publishing, 2006.

1. Stable growth during Edo era of Tokugawa Shogunate(1603-1867) which enabled many business start-ups.
2. Management competencies of families who started their own business in Edo era. Their competencies reached the level of perfection before the 18th century.
3. The philosophical context, with the 'Shingaku' education given in schools intended for the children of merchants, enabled the people to respect notions such as family unity, sense of commitment, willingness to engage in work, social obligations, etc.

Explanations by Susumu NOMURA, *Chozu Kigyo wa Nihon ni Ari* (Ancient Firms exist in Japan), Nihon Hoso Shupppan Kyokai (in Japanese), 2007.

1. A foreign country has never invaded Japan throughout history. In addition, Japan has never had a civil war that threatens all the territory as a whole.
2. The existence of a sense of respect that places greater emphasis on business sustainability than on kinship ties. This is why there was a time in Japanese family business when a non-family member could be appointed as chairman in order to liaise with the successor from the family. There are further cases where the president drawn from the family resigns his seat for his son-in-law. This mostly happens in companies located in Kansai region.
3. The existence of a culture and a long tradition of respect for manufacturing.
4. The ability (a)to adapt to environmental change, (b)to understand environmental change and (c) to maintain their core competencies.

(Katsuyuki KAMEI, Teruo SHINATO and Leo-Paul DANA, "International convergence and divergence on family entrepreneurship problems: the case of family firms in Japan" *International Journal of Entrepreneurship and Small Business*, Vol.30, Issue4, 2017)

Chapter 4
Health Management and Risk Management

Case 3. Company's Approach Centered on "Health Training Hall" Sunstar Inc. (Japan)

Introduction

The theme of "health" tends to have the impression that individuals should take care of it themselves; so, some readers may feel there is a difference between health and enterprise risk management. However, the activities of a company are the total of the activities of the people constituting the company. Therefore, if the corporate culture and way of thinking do not promote good health, it could become a big risk for the corporation. Recently, it is well understood as common sense that the maintenance of good health of employees has a high cost advantage.

- Sunstar Inc. established a "Health Training Hall" in order to avoid the risk of employees with poor health.
- The company was highly evaluated by society, and it was designated as an "Outstanding Health Management Corporation" in 2017., 2018 and 2019.
- It is dedicated to the development of oral care, including at the time of disaster, using its product-development technology.

1   Avoid Risk of Health of its Employees as a Company

Sunstar Group is a leading maker of oral care products, cosmetics, health food products, industrial adhesives, as well as other products. The company was established in 1932. Initially, the focus of the business was bicycle parts. It was selling adhesive for repairing flat bicycle tires filled in metal tubes. It started the production and sales of toothpaste in metal tubes by diverting the production facility, and since then, it has expanded its business area up to the present day. The name of the company was changed to Sunstar in 1950, a combined word of sun and star in the hope to be fresh by brushing teeth in the morning (sun) and at night (star). Kunio Kaneda, Sunstar's founder, suddenly died of diabetes at the young age of 50. As a result, a new company policy of "Company always dedicates itself to the improvement of public health and a culture of livelihood" was created in 1963. At the same time, it held out the policy of "Advance mental and physical health" in eight spirits in the moral code of conduct for employees from the way of thinking that "The employees engaged in the health industry should be in good health."

Hiroo Kaneda, the son of the founder and current chairman, also got sick from diabetes; however, he has now recovered from it thanks to a dietary therapy of brown rice and vegetables. He wanted to use his personal experience for the health maintenance of employees, and established "Sunstar Mental and Physical Health Training Hall" in 1985, an in-house welfare facility where health guidance, such as the prevention of metabolic syndrome and diabetes, can be provided for company employees. The top management of the company took measures against the impending hazard without overlooking it, and made an active effort to avoid the risk to employees as a company. This behavior should be highly evaluated regarding a company's risk management.

2 Accommodation-type Guidance in Order to Regain Health Balance

The health diagnostic menu for the employees of this company consists of an internal diagnosis, which is similar to that of an ordinary thorough medical checkup, together with a dental checkup. Those who are regarded as requiring a follow-up observation as a result have interviews with a doctor or health nurse, and six months later, a blood examination and other necessary checks will be conducted again. In this way, the company makes an effort to enhance employees' health consciousness and prevent the onset of disease. Furthermore, those who require specific health guidance can receive positive support in the form of an accommodation-type health guidance program at "Sunstar Mental and Physical Health Training Hall. According to this company, this is an accommodation-type health guidance program for two nights and three days to regain health balance from three perspectives of "diet," "body," and "consciousness," combined with learning about health, learning through reflecting on life-style, guidance of oral care, diet of brown rice and vegetables, exercises such as walking, aqua-aerobics, balance stretching, and hot and cold water bathing[1].

The expenses are borne by the Health Insurance Association of the company, and the days spent for this program are treated as a business trip and each department positively sends off its staff for it. It was 2007 when the

Health Management and Risk Management   31

accommodation-type health guidance program started. The number of those who were deemed required to participate in the health guidance was 170, and 120 out of them actually participated in the guidance. Since then, the number of trainees in the guidance program has been decreasing, which clearly shows the degree of health of employees by numbers.

This approach by the company is highly evaluated by society, and it was designated as an "Outstanding Health Management Corporation" in 2017, which was instituted by the "Ministry of Economy, Trade and Industry" and "Japan Health Conference." It also started a business selling foods like Japanese vegetable drinks, which are based on the diet of brown rice and vegetables, and other products provided in the Health Training Hall with the brand of "Health Training Hall." As a pioneering company that has spread the consciousness of "Health is the Value of Company" throughout the company, further activities are expected in the future.

3 Advocate Risk Management by Oral Care.

The company has been advocating the importance of oral care to the general public based upon the knowledge gained by the technical development of products. It is possible to prevent diseases and general conditions caused by periodontal disease by keeping the mouth clean; so, it can be said that it is risk management from the perspective of diseases.

The company also is taking an approach to enhance the awareness of the importance of oral care at the time of disaster. It becomes difficult to brush teeth regularly due to interruptions in water supply and evacuation at times of disaster and it increases the risk that the elderly, in particular, can contract aspiration pneumonia. Therefore, specifically, they stress the importance of preserving sets for oral care in disaster survival kits, and is developing simple methods of oral care for cases when there is no oral care set at the time of disaster. In a practical example, during the event of the Kumamoto Earthquake in 2016, they contributed liquid dentifrice which did not need water for rinsing the mouth, as a relief supply. Since then, the company has continued to persuade autonomous bodies to stockpile for disaster and delivered leaflets to their associate companies to promote use of the kits.

Employees are a driving force of the business development of the company, and labor quantity is proportional to sales volume in some industries. However, as overwork has been seen as a problem for some time, it is true that overwork raises health risks. Speaking in the short term, it comes down to a choice between the sales volume of the company and employee' health.

However, in the long view, there is no doubt in that "the health of employees leads to the development of the company." For example, if an employee takes time off work because of illness, it becomes necessary to ensure the working power to complement that of the employee. If the employee is to retire from work, there is a risk that a new employee must be recruited and educated from scratch. Furthermore, even if it does not lead to the stage of negatively impacting health, the importance of employee' health is obvious when pursuing operational efficiency, new business ideas, and the fulfillment of communication among employees. Not preoccupied with the follow-up of injuries and diseases, it is indispensable to incorporate preventive medicine and deal with the health of employees for business activities in the future.

Note:

1) Sunstar WEB site "Sunstar was designated to Outstanding Health Management Corporation in 2017" http://jp.sunstar.com/company/press/2017/022l.html
"The Suntory Group believes health is not something simply related to hospitals but also satisfies health of both body and mind, energy in everyday work, and enthusiasm. We started health management from 2016 to promote an even greater level of health for our employees and their families based on this belief."
https://www.suntory.com/csr/activity/diversity/health/

Exercise:

Describe health management in your organization.

Chapter 5
Natural Disasters and Risk Management (1)
Crisis Management and Leadership in March 11.

Case 4. Leadership shown at "TEDxTohoku" (Japan)

Introduction

Japan is one of the countries where natural disasters occur most frequently and seriously. Earthquakes have especially been great threats and enormous damage has been brought to Japan throughout its history. Tremendous earthquakes, which are regarded on a one-in-a-hundred scale, have recently occurred one after another in Japan. There are apprehensions where a huge earthquake originating in the Nankai Trough or an earthquake right under an urban area, such as Tokyo, will strike in the near future. Therefore, it is definitely a key to the business continuity for an enterprise to undergo appropriate risk management.

- The Great Hanshin Earthquake Disaster, which was an inland earthquake directly below an urban area in 1995, forced many enterprises to prepare countermeasures against earthquakes.
- However, the Great East Japan Earthquake in 2011 brought unanticipated damages, and many enterprises were unable to draw on their lessons to take effective measures against the disaster.
- How a leader performs their leadership role in the aftermath of a disaster influences subsequent risk management.

1 Great East Japan Earthquake and TEDxTohoku

Recognition has been widely settled since the Great East Japan Earthquake that an earthquake repeats, and we must learn from history. In the term "risk management," it is essential to identify and assess risks, taking past situations into account. Furthermore, it is also vital in risk management to observe and examine scenarios toward the restoration following a disaster. This section presents

"TEDxTohoku," which was produced by students of the School of Engineering, Tohoku University with collective effort for the Great East Earthquake Recovery.

Technology, Entertainment, Design (TED) is a media organization for presentation events in the United States of America, which has been well-known worldwide and has attracted an increasing number of viewers on video websites these days. A speech event at "TEDxTohoku" was held in the disaster-stricken area of the Tohoku region. This was even established with a concept to send messages to the world, such as what has been learned and realized through the process to overcome and rebuild following the disaster, and ideas or stories, which are characteristic of Tohoku. Lecturers ascending the platform of the "TEDxTohoku 2011" event were representative members playing an active part of various fields in the damaged area. This section introduces two lecturers of the event.

2 Hideko Oikawa, Oikawa Denim

Oikawa Denim has gained an excellent reputation for technical strength as a made-in-Japan product, although low-priced denim products or jeans made overseas prevail in the market. This company established an original brand with the world's first denim fabric with hemp yarn woven texture.

Fig. 5.1 TEDxTohoku 2011 (Hideko Oikawa, Oikawa Denim)

Natural Disasters and Risk Management (1)   35

Oikawa Denim was once located in Kesennuma City but the factory was moved to an uptown area. Thus, the building of the factory narrowly escaped being damaged. However, the houses of Oikawa and employees and the facilities, except for the factory, were swept away by the tsunami tidal waves. Oikawa offered the factory on the upland to people as an evacuation shelter. It was only one month later from the disaster when Oikawa Denim resumed operation with a generated emergency electric power source.

A powerful symbol for the restoration was found in woods forty days after the disaster. The hope for the recovery was a pair of jeans from Oikawa Denim, which had been stored in a warehouse. With the store house carried away by a tsunami, after a long journey, the jeans were found to have no loose threads. "Denim products can be patched up when they are worn out. Denim products can be washed when they become dirty with mud. Humans can stand up to live a life again when we collapse. We can stand up whenever we collapse," said Hideko Oikawa. Deep empathy was shared by all the participants in the event hall.

3 Kazuie Iinuma, Ishinomaki Red Cross Hospital

Ishinomaki Red Cross Hospital was the only hospital that was undamaged and not flooded during the East Japan Earthquake in Ishinomaki City. The hospital provided medical care to many residents and offered an evacuation site after the disaster. The risk management of this hospital served as the reason that the hospital survived the inundation. They had prepared unexpected disasters to strike.

For tangible elements such as construction, the hospital had been built with a foundation raised three meters, based on the research which examined the history of overflowing of the Kitagami River. Seismic isolation structures were also employed to prevent damage. The basements of the hospital were equipped with a yard, which was intended to receive relief supplies in emergency. The waiting area was designed to be changed into a space for a treatment area. For intangible elements, study and training, and earthquake drills were conducted determinedly and also trainings with a helicopter were performed.

These risk managements procedures with advance preparation enabled amazingly agile responses to the disaster. Only four minutes after the great earthquake, disaster headquarters were established. Triage area setup was complete, and doctors were assigned. It could be said that "However much you prepare, something unanticipated would happen." However, Ishinomaki Red Cross Hospital proved that preparation can provide an appropriate response.

Fig. 5.2 The first TEDxTohoku cooperatively produced by students in the Tohoku region for recovery from the tsunami.

Exercise:

Watch one of the TEDxTohoku videos on youtube and discuss it.

Chapter 6
Natural Disasters and Risk Management (2)

Case 5. Kumamoto Earthquakes and the Business
Continuity Planning (BCP) (Japan)

Introduction

The number of enterprises which have started establishing BCP following the Great East Earthquake has increased.

When the 2016 Kumamoto Earthquakes occurred, enterprises which had learned from the Great East Earthquake to prepare countermeasures such as the establishment of BCP, were able to recover swiftly.

BCP leads to the improvement of corporate vision, management strategy, and enterprise value in a community.

1   The 2016 Kyushu-Kumamoto Earthquakes

The aftershocks of the Great East Japan Earthquake continued to occur into 2017 as of the time of the writing of Japanese version of this book. Aftershocks happen every few days, weeks, or even after more than six years have passed since an earthquake struck. The background for this book is that a massive earthquake occurred in the Kyushu region in 2016. That is, the 2016 Kyushu-Kumamoto Earthquakes. This disaster was a series of earthquakes, or swarm earthquakes. Two earthquakes with a seismic intensity of seven occurred, the foreshock on April 14, 2016 and the main shock on April 16, 2016. Later, two earthquakes with seismic intensity in the upper six range and three earthquakes with a seismic intensity lower than six followed the first two earthquakes within a very short time. Firm buildings had collapsed, which were supposed to be resistant to an earthquake, but were unable to endure repeated and vigorous shakings. Although no shock over a broad area, nor a tsunami occurred the northern areas of Kumamoto Prefecture and Oita Prefecture were stricken and severely damaged.

Risk management can be reinforced via examination of a hazard. After overcoming a hazard, potential future hazards must be identified in order to take countermeasures against further risks. This section introduces several enterprises which were meant to avoid as many damages as possible in the Kumamoto Earthquakes, as risk management was reinforced with the examination of knowledge gained after overcoming the Great East Japan Earthquake.

2 Success with BCP established as a lesson of earthquake disasters: Renesas Electronics Corporation

Renesas Electronics Corporation, a semiconductor maker, was extraordinarily successful in production recovery following the Kumamoto Earthquakes. It was only one week after the disaster when Renesas Electronics Corporation resumed production, after having suffered the most intensive seismic level of seven of the Kumamoto Earthquakes. Originally, the semiconductor industry was vulnerable to earthquakes, because in nanotechnology manufacturing, circuits on the scale of one/one billion are being produced (0.000 000 001 m). In the Great East Japan Earthquake, Renesas Electronics Corporation had a bitter experience, where a factory located in Naka, Ibaraki Prefecture was severely damaged and had to stop production for about three months.

Renesas Electronics thoroughly reconsidered BCP after the Great East Japan Earthquake to formulate a crisis management system in case of damages from natural disasters, other than earthquakes, including tsunami, inundation, and volcanic eruption. Renesas Electronics Corporation intended to build factories minimizing the negative impacts of a crisis and maximizing the ability to resume production after a crisis. For tangible elements, seismic upgrading of buildings was enforced. For intangible elements, risk countermeasures were focused on sharing information rapidly. Risk information, such as influences on supply and stock, with recommended standards in an emergency was shared with customers. They requested that some makers share the commonization of the semiconductor production system and reconsider excessively small volume production of great varieties. Further, rules for business partners were formulated: "to announce damage conditions within twenty-four hours after a natural disaster" and "to resume production within one week."

In the 2016 Kumamoto Earthquakes, the Kawajiri factory located in Kumamoto City, was able to reduce damages to production equipment. The factory fortunately had completed seismic reinforcement up to the level of seismic intensity in the upper six range by the end of 2013, including quake-free functions on production equipment. Through these efforts, Renesas Electronics Corporation resumed production sequentially on April 22, 2016, on the eighth day after the first earthquake. They are considering sharing their BCP with subcontractors and associated plants in the near future.

3 Plans to reconsider BCP and practice drills for future operation after suffering damages to production plants during the Kumamoto Earthquakes: Sony Corporation

Sony Corporation had a production plant located 20 km away from the epicenter. This factory was a major base production plant for camera image sensors, which had been prepared for an earthquake and other natural disasters for a long time via formulating a BCP. However, the impacts of the Kumamoto Earthquakes were more devastating than they had anticipated. Plant buildings were heavily damaged so that workers were unable to even enter the buildings. It took two weeks to be able to enter the plants. Walls and ceilings were broken and semiconductor wafers were scattered inside of the buildings.

Judging from the degree of damage the factory was not expected to be able to resume full operation until after the summer. In fact, the plants were able to operate at full capacity by the end of July, one month before the planned date thanks to support from business connections and reinforcement work on the buildings. The volume of delivery was restored to a normal level before the subsequent earthquakes at the end of September.

Sony Corporation announced in October that they would reconsider BCP after examining the sequence of events. They would formulate a plan for the system to enable a restart within two months even facing a natural disaster crisis. Their concrete measures were to reconsider a storage system for semiconductor wafers to halt damages of goods in process, and to readjust items in a check list for a quick recovery and restart of product operations. In addition, production bases would be deployed in several locations, and distribution stock would be increased as countermeasures. Furthermore, it was determined that training programs were conducted for potential natural disasters.

4 Quicker recovery than Kyushu Electric Power, utilizing generator vehicles inside and outside the company: Tokyo Ohka Kogyo Co., Ltd.

Tokyo Ohka Kogyo Co., Ltd. manufactures materials for liquid crystal display. The company had damage to the Aso plant during the Kumamoto Earthquakes. Four plant buildings had been designed with light ceilings for risk management. The plant used organic solvent in production, and applied to the Fire Services Act as a dangerous object manufacturing factory. Therefore, the plants were built with light ceilings to vent the shock of an explosion up to the ceilings and to minimize damage to the surrounding area.

The Aso area, which the plant was located in, was close to the epicenter observed with the magnitude seven earthquake, and later was the epicenter of aftershocks. Despite these strong shakings, the damage to the Aso plant of Tokyo Ohka Kogyo was limited to some parts of the ceilings. Their preparation efforts in risk management were fruitful. The buildings were designed as a factory for dangerous object manufacturing according to the law. In addition they employed an inspection system for the mounting parts of tanks and pipes after the Great East Japan Earthquake.

Tokyo Ohka Kogyo managed to overcome the challenge of a quick recovery. The Aso area suffered from a huge scale landslide after the earthquakes, which induced the deconstruction of steel tower power-transmission lines. Under these circumstances, this company swiftly established an emergency headquarters for all regular chief directors and estimated the quantity of electricity required for product operation on April 16, 2016 when the magnitude seven earthquake occurred. Generator vehicles were gathered at the Aso plant from other branches of the company nationwide. Based on the estimation that more electricity was needed for temperature control, they requested cooperative companies in the Kyushu region to lend Generator vehicles. Through these struggles, Tokyo Ohka Kogyo was able to resume operation on April 25, 2016, three days ahead of the restart of the electricity supply by Kyushu Electric Power Co., Inc.

This successful response owed a great deal to the lessons learned from the Great East Japan Earthquake. The Sagami branch plant in Kanagawa Prefecture had experienced a planned power outage, which was conducted by the electric company after the Great East Japan Earthquake. The manufacturing system of the company had a great deal of production processes requiring temperature control. Tokyo Ohka Kogyo prepared and formulated a BCP plan themselves, to ensure electricity for a risk of power outage, which could cause a one week delay in recovery. This reaction by Tokyo Ohka Kogyo was reported in the mass media and contributed to the establishment of BCP in other companies.

Trace of Natural Disaster

Fig. 6.1 Kumamoto Castle (February 2017), photograph by Katsuyuki Kamei

Fig. 6.2 Nagatoro Elementary School, Miyagi Prefecture (August 2011), photograph by Katsuyuki Kamei

Exercise:

What is a lesson from the Great Japan East Earthquake on March 11, 2011?

Column 4: Top Management Risk, most difficult internal risk to prevent

The late Konosuke Matsushita, founder of Panasonic once said "A company is its people." The biggest risk for a company starting a business is a management risk.

The management risk lies in the situation where top executives are deficient of the qualities for business, risk sensitivity, decisiveness, and leadership, which results in loose management.

The personality and the capability of top executives can negatively affect the achievement of the company. In the worst case, they might cause a corporate scandal or a bankruptcy. The biggest management risk lies in the situations where the executive lacks decision making capability.

Case of Daio Paper Corporation (Japan)

This is a scandal which attacked the paper manufacturing company taking the third place in Japan.

Daio Paper Corporation, whose executives took advantage of their position for their own self-interest. This case is related to the aggravated breach of trust case where the top executive privatized the company to appropriate the money.

The base of the problem lies in the fact that the founder had taken hold of great power within the company since its establishment, and there should be a corporate re-organization.

Case of Toshiba (Japan)

Toshiba reported the largest losses among Japanese enterprises due to the accounting fraud problems that came into the open one after another. Illegally loaned more than one billion yen. There were also some problems with the accounting auditor.

The scandal by Toshiba was generally recognized in Feb, 2015.

The beginning of the scandal was related to the accounting fraud. The top executive of Toshiba demanded the manipulation of the sales and profit figures so that the corporate performance looks better. In the same year, they declared the huge impairment due to the acquisition of U.S company, Westinghouse (WH). The risk of nuclear business which was not noticed, due to its profit margins. The huge losses related to WH. Among the multiple risks including the corporate structure and the changing market, the biggest risk can be said to lie in the executive himself.

The accounting fraud case of the company, which used to be called an honor company for its corporate management. The accounting frauds were disclosed one after another, with the modified amount of money exceeding 200 billion yen.

The company was on the verge of a crisis of delisting from the stock market. The process Toshiba focused on the immediate performance, while defending its own interest. The responsibility of the top executive. The biggest corporate risk is that which comes from the executives.

Chapter 7
Risk Taking: "Avoid" or "Retain"

Case 6. Renault Espace (France)

Introduction

There is not a decision without a risk.

We tend to think that "a risk" is a negative element for a company, a risk has the potential to damage a company's profit. However, seen from the risk management field, it is considered to be positive. For example, there is an idea of "risk taking," meaning that the company expands / develops the business by purposely taking a risk. Of course, there might be a case where there is a loss of profit resulting from the risk taking. Therefore, it is necessary to deal with unexpected matters by foreseeing the worst possible scenario.

1 Renault's decision to launch the joint development of a new car and the result of risk taking

Renault took a risk to create "Espace," the first minivan in Europe
- Whether to "avoid" a risk caused by developing an original new product or to "take it"
- Positive and negative of two cases: Peugeot which shunned a risk and Renault which took it

Renault[1] is one of the largest car manufacturers in Europe with its worldwide brand name, in terms of the size involving subsidiary companies. The company founded by Louis Renault enjoyed its 120th anniversary. The former representative, Carlos Ghosn who once restored Nissan Motor, got arrested in Tokyo in November 2018. Needless to say, Renault has been involved in developing a variety of new cars. However, the development of the first minivan in Europe, "Espace" is one of the topic subjects Renault has experienced.

The company which recommended that Renault develop Espace was Matra

Automobile (hereafter mentioned as Matra) which was the largest car manufacturer after Renault and PSA Peugeot Citroën. Matra was established in 1964 by Jean-Luc Lagardère, who took a lead in a variety of industries relating to space, aviation and defense. Marta, at first, was primarily manufacturing sports cars.

In the beginning of 1984, Matra was seeking to develop a new type of car targeting the family class. It was the "minivan" which was a vehicle with a higher height and enabled the driver to drive without suffering from stress even for long distances, and had the capacity to carry more luggage.

Matra, first approached Peugeot about the joint development of a new car model. However, Peugeot decided not to "take a risk," thinking that "this car model will not sell because of its novelty." Then, Matra approached Renault. Unlike Peugeot, Renault decided to "take a risk" and participated in the joint development. In this way, Espace was born.

2 Monopolized the minivan market in Europe

In cooperation with Matra, Renault launched the production of Espace. The car bodies were produced by Matra which utilized its original processing technology for plastics, while machine parts were produced by Renault. The new car was completed by putting the separate parts together.

The body being processed by use of plastics reduced the production cost, which made profitable low-volume production possible. After the sales in 1984, the minivan market which the French called "monospace" appeared, and it continued developing until the beginning of 1990s, having no equal. Thus, Renault and Matra monopolized the European minivan market.

Peugeot which avoided taking a risk, missed a big business opportunity. It took Peugeot ten years to develop its own minivans by themselves and to enter into the minivan market. Peugeot had to cooperate with Italian manufacturer Fiat, in order to enter the minivan market. It was a case that showed that avoiding a risk resulted in losing potential profit.

3 Matra had to shut-down despite its strategic success

Starting in 2001, when Espace was updated to its fourth model version with great success, Renault moved the production line for car bodies into its own factories, in order to start producing iron car bodies instead of using Matra's

Risk Taking: "Avoid" or "Retain"   45

plastics processing. In other words, Renault launched independent production of Espace.

Then, Matra started production of Renault's "Avantime" which had a futuristic design, in place of the Espace. However, Avantime was not widely accepted in the market and sales went down. As a result, in February 2001, the Lagardère Group who ran Matra had to announce its withdrawal from the car manufacturing market. On March 14th, half a month after the withdrawal announcement, Lagadère died. The group was succeeded by Lagardere's son Arnaud, and is presently involved in not only Air Bus business, but also in the publication business, media, and book distribution as a leading French enterprise group. In addition, Matra was later sold to an Italian car manufacturer and is now in charge of R&D of automobiles by the name of Matra Automobile Engineering.

4   Speculative risks should be taken after sufficient investigation/estimation

Viewing the above case from the point of risk management, it can be said that Peugeot took the decision to avoid risks by refusing the joint development with Matra. It was the simplest way of risk avoidance among other risk controls. On the other hand, Renault accepted the offer. It was "risk taking," the opposite of avoidance.

In general, due to the image of the word, we tend to consider risk avoiding the most important thing. However, considering the case of Peugeot, to avoid risks can be said to be negative risk treatment (risk handling). As previously mentioned, it might lead to the abandonment of potential profits. Therefore, it is essential for leaders or executives to not easily dismiss risk taking.

Apart from this, considering that Renault's decision was based on the sufficient consideration of risks, it can be called speculative risk taking. Based on the fact that this decision is literally "speculative," it is necessary to take risks after conducting sufficient investigation/confirmation as well as evaluation/ analysis regarding whether it becomes a business chance or not.

These days especially, we will face many situations where we have to take speculative risks, irrespective of the size of companies or the domain of businesses. There are three bases for the decision of taking risks, or not:

whether it is "a risk we can take responsibility for"
whether it is "a risk we cannot take responsibility for"
what will happen if we do not take the risk.

We conclude this chapter by showing the example of Universal Studio Japan. When Universal Studio Japan with the three slogans:

Decide Now. Do it now
Everything is possible
Swing the bat!

was enjoying 70 billion yen in sales, it decided to take the risk of investing 45 billion yen to produce the Harry Potter Area. On the other hand, it decided not to take the risk to produce a second park in Okinawa. The prosperity of USJ after this is just as we see today.

Fig. 7.1 Renault Espace (February 2005, photograph by Katsuyuki Kamei)

Note:

1) Renault is an automobile manufacturer with a head office in Paris, France. It'was founded in 1898, by the Renault brothers. It is the largest automobile company in Europe when including the parent company, Nissan in 2017.

Exercise:

Explain your own experience of 'avoid' or 'retain' type risk taking.

Chapter 8
Safety and Risk Management in Sports Events
- Case of Citizen Marathons in Japan -

Case 7. Japanese Citizens' Marathon

Introduction

Purpose and Importance of Research on Risk Management and Safety Management in Marathon Races

In Japan, Marathon and road racing events have surged in number and participation. This running boom was triggered by the first Tokyo Marathon in 2007. The total number of citizen marathon and road race runners has increased to eight million, and the number of marathons and road races exceeds one hundred and sixty for the races authorized by the Japan Association of Athletics Federations (JAAF) and sixteen hundred for both authorized and not authorized races by the JAAF. Needless to say, participation in the races promotes the health of runners. The "Isumi Kenkoh Marathon," highlights that the marathon race has contributed to regional vitalization. The "Osaka Marathon" provides cases where the urban-style marathon has offered opportunities to mature a new type of sports culture and has contributed to tourism.

However, we must consider that the running boom involves an increase in risks along with the increase of citizen marathon races. Running marathons is a difficult sport and accidents related to the health of runners do not cease during a race. Furthermore, unanticipated incidents could occur in spite of administrative management, e.g. the Boston Marathon bombing terrorist attack which occurred near the race end point on April 15, 2013. Therefore, risk management is necessary both for the runner and the organizer.

1　Review on Safety and Risk Management of Marathons

Runners must manage their health and train on a daily basis as well as on the day of the race. Organizers of marathons must conduct diversified risk managements and safety managements such as arranging the administrators, the police, and the local community, including residents around the marathon course, and also do their best to ensure the safety of the runners[1]. According to "*Shimin Marason/Rodo Reisu Unei Gaidorain,*" "Citizen Marathon/Road Race Management Guideline" provided by the Japan Association of Athletics Federations (JAAF), points of consideration are as follows:

Six Points of consideration in Marathon Races; items of risk management

1. Preparation of the race in advance for runners
    (1) physical condition management (2) nutrition guidance/water supply
    (3) countermeasures against adverse weather
    (4) implementation of a jogging class
    (5) propriety of the use of costume or electronic devices
    (6) strict punctuality of the arrival in the race site/responses to delay
2. General management
    (1) items to be written in the marathon race guidelines
    (2) conditions to notify runners of before the start
    (3) services provided by the marathon organization
    (4) emergency contact system
3. Marathon course setting
    (1) start point and finish point
    (2) overall conditions of the course (traffic regulation notices to residents and spectators, ensuring the safety of the course, ensuring the safety of pedestrians crossing support at the course and the road, strict regulation of the time limit at checkpoints, and ensuring a route for emergency transportation)
    (3) preparation of the course (i water supply, ii food supply, iii lavatory, iv waste disposal)
4. Medical counterplans
    (1) establishment of a medical committee   (2) lifesaving training sessions
    (3) first-aid stations   (4) automated external defibrillator (AED)
    (5) system of emergency transportation and procedures of request for ambulances
5. Measures against weather

(1) measures against heat　(2) measures against rain
(3) temporary evacuation measures in rough weather or a natural disaster
(4) methods of transmission and guidance
6. Officials and volunteers
   (1) preparation prior to the marathon race　(2) appropriate number of staff
   (3) allocation of roles for officials and volunteers
   (4) recruitment of officials and volunteers
   (5) responses to complaints and requests

2　Case Study (1) : Isumi Kenkoh Marathon

The Isumi Kenkoh Marathon, the Akemi Masuda Cup, has continuously gained high acclaim from the first race in December of 2008 to the present. According to a survey of "RUNNET," which conducts marathon ranking based on popular vote by runners, "Marathon ranking in 2015"announced that the Isumi Kenkoh Marathon earned sixth place in the department of total evaluation ranking, first in the department of scale in between three thousand and seven thousand participants, first in the department of event of half marathon, and second in the department of distance of ten km. Furthermore, the Isumi Kenkoh Marathon was certified as one of the "Hundred Road Races in Japan in 2015" by the editorial department of Runnet/R-bies sports foundation in April of 2015. That is the Isumi Kenkoh Marathon has been chosen as one of the hundred Japanese representative road races among two thousand exciting marathons and road races.

Safety, Risk and Insurance Management in the Isumi Kenkoh Marathon: Measures of Prevention of Accidents

1. Insurance
   (1) participants: accident insurance, injury and disease compensation (solatium)
   (2) officials: accident insurance
   * covered by the Japan Association of City Mayors Comprehensive Insurance in City and Board of Education Mutual Aid Association
2. Preparation for the race start of elementary school children
   (1) form school children into a line in the order of their bib number (a bib number is assigned to a child referring to last year time record and target time), and to leave sufficient space between children
   (2) brief the children on points of attention before the race starts, e.g. check shoes laces and prohibited matters, do not push the runner in front or run off

the runner on the side

3. Running direction
    (1) participants must follow staff instruction; immediately after the start, run on the left side and make right-handed turns at the turning back point
    (2) staff and color cones are placed around the water stations to prevent backtracking

4. Water supply station
    Every water station prepares "water" and "sports drink" (measures against dehydration)
    (1) main site: one station　(2) five km race: one station; ten km race: two stations
    (3) half marathon: six stations (two stations with chocolate and banana offered)

5. First-aid station and rescue staff
    (1) the rescue headquarters: the main site
    (2) first-aid station: two stations (ten km race and half marathon: around 3.5 km, half marathon: around 7.5 km)
    (3) bicycle AED unit: around the goal point and along the marathon course
    (4) small-sized electric car unit (Q car unit): along the marathon course
    (5) rescue cars: three

6. Rescue equipment
    measures against hyperthermia and dehydration: oral rehydration solution and sufficient sports drink
    measures against hypothermia: immediate transportation and supply of blankets and towels

7. Rescue staff (in the 2015 marathon race)
    total number of staff: 87 members (the first day: 13 members, the second day: 74 members)
    (1) one doctor and three nurses
    (2) thirteen city employees (nine public health nurses and four regular city employees)
    (3) International Budo University trainer team: forty-one members
    (4) broad area fire-fighting employees: twenty members
    (5) Q-car unit: nine members

8. Rescue meeting
    (1) general meeting: conducted three times
    (2) meeting of each group: conducted three times

Safety and Risk Management in Sports Events 51

3 Case Study (2) : Safety Management of the Marathon Race at Osaka Marathon

The rescue system for the Osaka Marathon, which has thirty thousand runners participating, is basically constructed as follows:
1) Implementation of a safe environment for the marathon
2) Prevention in advance of accidents and prevention of extended accidents
3) Introduction of a triage system for runners, others, and the provision of emergency treatment

The Osaka Marathon has been provided with medical services by the Osaka Medical association since the first race in 2011. This association, with cooperation from the Osaka Clinical Orthopaedic Association, dispatches fifty orthopedists and twenty sport physicians certified by the Japan Medical Association as medical and rescue staff. The sixth Osaka Marathon in 2016 did not have any grave cases even though thirteen emergency transportations occurred and the number of people who utilized the first-aid stations was 1,410. It is recognized that the staff, who work from the early morning, also need to be paid attention to for their health management. ("The Journal of Osaka Medical Association" of January of 2017)

4 Case Study (3) : Kashiwa no ha marathon

The fourth Kashiwa No Ha Soukai Marathon was organized by the Earth run club on May the 3rd, 2016 (Tuesday, national holiday) at Kashiwanoha park stadium, Chiba prefectural institution (photographed by Katsuyuki Kamei)

At the reception, we saw a paper saying that "a written pledge and a questionnaire concerning the condition of health" to be completed and submitted, with comprehensive instruction provided by the staff of the Earth run club, the organizer of the marathon race and water absorption sponges for a measure against heat. Water stations were provided by the organizer, and various kinds of fluids supplied by runners.

The organizer, Earth run club carries out drastic safety management. It is called the "Three, five, and seven system for emergency in safety management"

That means as follows,

when an emergency occurs there are:

three minutes to report (collection of the first report)

five minutes to dispatch (safety committee member or medical staff)

seven minutes to first-aid (AED and call for an ambulance)

Water stations and staff are stationed in places to enable the three, five, and seven minutes system. The first thing to do is to determine, after several trials of running, a course for participants to run smoothly. The organizers determine the running route, in that they themselves run through as a race participant.
(Information provided by Earth run club/event information center and the NPO Corporation Japan Out fitness Society)

5 Case Study (4) : Anti-terrorism measures and disaster management at the Tokyo Marathon

5.1 Anti-terrorism

The tenth Tokyo Marathon was held on February the 28th, 2016. The Metropolitan Police Department and the Tokyo Marathon Foundation have had apprehension on "Soft Targets" for terrorism, which would attack civilian sites where people congregate in large numbers like November 2015 Paris attacks. They guarded the tenth Tokyo Marathon with strict alert with more than ten thousand security members, which was the largest in scale ever in the past. On the day before the event, February the 27th of 2016, rescue members and police dogs from the Metropolitan Police Department searched for suspicious objects in front of the Tokyo government office building around the start point area of the race.

The measures are as follows.
-Confirmation of bib numbers (number cards) and security inspection
-Collection of bottles; no pet bottles allowed
-Strict regulation of allowable and prohibited items into the start zone and the course area
-Security check for carry-on luggage at the gate to enter the start zone
-Security check for personal belongings at the gate to enter the start zone
-"The important race information of Tokyo Marathon 2016"

The Metropolitan Police Department have enforced a counter-terrorism strategy called "to have a visible security force presence" to deter soft target attacks. State-of-the-art technologies from the private sector were introduced. The number of police running was increased from sixty members in the previous event to ninety members to operate the rescue system for emergencies or sickness. Metal detector security devices were increased in number to assist the enforcement of baggage inspections.

Interception drones have been introduced for the first time to capture a drone in the air if a radio-controlled drone comes to disturb the race. Specialized units called "Interceptor Drone Team (IDT) were assigned to watch and wait in several places. Scouting from the air above the Big Sight at the finish point is conducted with camera-mounted drones and airships by private sectors to monitor the situations on the ground. Police officers go on patrols riding a Segway which is a two-wheeled, self-balancing scooter to stand on for riding.[2]

5.2 Countermeasures for earthquakes

"The important information for all participants of the Tokyo Marathon 2016" including matters of attentions in the "Action manual (Earthquake)" and "MAP of evacuation zones for runners and temporary stay facilities in Tokyo" showed countermeasures for natural disasters such as earthquakes.

- If the strong vibration of an earthquake is felt:
  If an earthquake with a seismic intensity of five or more occurs in Tokyo, this marathon race will be terminated by the judgment of the organizers. When you feel a strong vibration, or when event staffs in the course announce it, you must not push yourself but abandon running to confirm the circumstances.
- Standby places after stopping running:
- To follow instructions of the event staffs in the course, after stopping running
- To wait at the standby place, as a general rule, until the event staff announces instructions.
- Not to stay around the center of the running course but to move to the side of the course, so emergency vehicles can pass through.
- If you get injured or see someone get injured:
  To contact an event staff member close to you
- Belongings during the race:
  To participate in the race, having a smart phone or a cellular phone for emergency contact for returning home, and an IC card for public transportation for emergency transportation for returning home is recommended.
- Precaution in mind
  ◊ It is recommended to check the Marathon "Disaster Prevention Website" provided by the Tokyo metropolitan government prior to event participation.
- Evacuation in an emergency
  In a case where an evacuation is required, the event staff will guide the runners to the evacuation site which was assigned beforehand according to the location

of the runner (the traveling point)

■ People who are unable to return home after disasters

For people who have trouble returning home, temporary stay facilities are prepared by the Tokyo Metropolitan Government.

(1) Tokyo Metropolitan Government Hall (Nishishinjuku, Shinjuku-ku) (2) Tokyo International Forum (Marunouchi, Chiyoda-ku) (3) Edo-Tokyo Museum (Yokoami, Sumida-ku) (4) Museum of Contemporary Art Tokyo (Miyoshi, Koto-ku) (5) Ariake Tennis Forest Park, tennis facilities (Ariake, Koto-ku) (6) Tokyo Big Sight (Ariake, Koto-ku)

("Participation Information for the Tokyo Marathon 2016" page 16-17)

6 Risk Management Customized for Individual Needs and Respect to People in the Work Sites of Safety Management

This paper provides viewpoints of risk management pertaining to citizen marathons and presents two key principles.

The first viewpoint is "risk management customized for individual needs." Individuals or organizations have their own characteristic identities as well as different circumstances of their marathon events in risk management as a runner or an organizer of a citizen marathon. Therefore, risk management must be practiced via examining reliable information or concepts and planning safety management suitable to their own individual needs or organizations. Thus, risk management can be performed with assurance.

In the real world, a condition cannot exist without a risk. In the case of citizen marathons, runners cannot escape from the risk of injury. Even if management organizations make every possible effort, they still have a risk of trouble. However, a risk could help humans grow. In the condition of a risk, both a runner and an organizer make efforts to overcome the risk. Consequently, individual running records and the quality of event management may improve and advance.

The second viewpoint is "social risk management." Social risk refers to a risk which has a great impact on the whole society, such as a natural disaster. The point is that for handling these sorts of risks, cooperative activity is necessary among households, local communities, enterprises and public administrations. This is the social management where the risk management must be conducted with social cooperation.

The Tokyo Marathon is credited with inspiring the running boom. Citizen

Safety and Risk Management in Sports Events   55

marathons could be referred to as a social phenomenon. Risks to citizen marathons involve social risks which must be treated with social cooperation. This requires a non-self-centered approach. The runner must not seek only for an immediate goal of "time record" without caring for others. The organizer of the running event must not give a priority on near-term interests or efficiency, thinking that "the purpose is only to make the event successful." It is imperative that local communities, public administrations, enterprises, schools, and households have a common understanding of risk management. Thus, the key for success must be to respect all the people supporting the marathon, including staff who plan and conduct safety management, staff who are in charge of guarding the event, volunteers who perform activities such as working at water stations and viewers who cheer runners along roadsides.

Note:

1) "*Shimin Marason / Rodo Reisu Unei Gaidorain*" "Citizen Marathon /Road Race Management Guideline", Public Interest Incorporated Foundation, Japan Association of Athletics Federations (JAAF) April the 1st, 2013, http://www.jaaf.or.jp/rikuren/pdf/road.pdf
References related to the Isumi Kenkoh Marathon: Marathon pamphlet, Information leaflet distributed at the race,Interview survey conducted at Isumi City hall on September the 9th, 2014. Resources based on Kazuyuki Tokoro of Shogai Gakushu ka in board of education of Isumi City
2) Documents provided by a newspaper, "Tokyo Shinbun, morning edition on February the 28th, 2016, on the day of the Tokyo Marathon Race)

Exercise:

Choose one entertainment event, sport, music, etc. and describe it from the viewpoint of risk management.

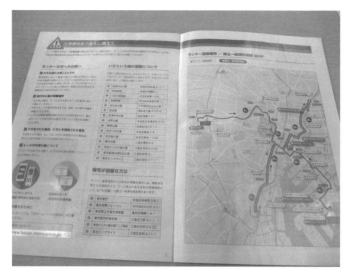

Fig. 8.1 Participation Information for the Tokyo Marathon 2016 (photograph by Katsuyuki Kamei)

Fig. 8.2 Q car in Isumi Kenkoh Marathon 2016 (photograph by Katsuyuki Kamei)

Safety and Risk Management in Sports Events

Fig. 8.3 A runner slipping by the rainfall at the Tokyo Marathon 2019 (photograph by Hiroshi Nagamatsu)

Fig. 8.4 Goal, London Marathon 2017 (photograph by Atsuo Sugimoto)

Fig. 8.5 Medical rescue, Berlin Marathon 2018 (photograph by Katsuyuki Kamei)

Fig. 8.6 'Risiken hinter sich lassen', 1km to the goal, Berlin Marathon 2018 (photograph by Katsuyuki Kamei)

Chapter 9
Interview

1 A Decision to retreat, and the courage to go forward
Advance Create Co., Ltd. President/Founder,
Yoshiharu Hamada

Advance Create Co., Ltd. was established in 1995. I felt that the deregulation of insurance agency business, which would be conducted the next year with the enforcement of the new Insurance Business Law, would provide a good business opportunity to enter this field. This enterprise started without publicity and potential customers. However, we drew the attention of customers with a unique strategy of fabricating and posting leaflets, which could not be imagined in today's internet society. Leaflets were distributed nationwide, and inquiries were sent to us by potential customers. We sold insurance via mail-order. There was no other company that employed this method at that time. However, with the business development of only this one model, I firmly believed that the mail-order system would gain popularity in the insurance industry. Advance Create Co., Ltd. became listed on NASDAQ Japan in the Osaka Stock Exchange(the name at that time) in 2002. It was the first time in Japan that an insurance specialized agency was listed.

Later, this enterprise began opening insurance stores to complement the mail-order system. The insurance shops increased in number to 200 nationwide in 2006. However, Advance Create experienced a decline in profits and a deficit for the first time since the stock became listed. At the same time, banks and commercial facilities, which had been cooperative with us in our expansion of branches, changed their attitude. Opinions in the firm were mostly that this company should make efforts to keep the shops the same as before. However, a proverb came to mind, saying "*Mikiri Senry;*" this Japanese proverb means "It is worth *senryo*, big money to determine to give up." Another proverb came to mind, saying "*Mo ha mada nari and mada ha mo nari*," which is used for forecasting market tendency. Translating the words, *mo* (already), is *mada* (yet), and *mada* (yet), is *mo* (already). This proverb means that when you think it has already reached the bottom, it is still going down and has not reached the bottom yet, and when you think it is still going up and has not hit the ceiling yet, it has hit the ceiling already. These sayings are derived from the Edo period. When the economic bubble burst, I saw many banks fall into bankruptcy. I decided to "cut off." The shops were reduced to twenty-three branches named "*Hoken Ichiba*" (Insurance Market). Advance Create pivoted towards the internet and returned profit the following year. Several years later, people around us came to highly value my decision from 2006.

There are two terms for management. One is "judgment" and the other is "decision." To judge is to gather diverse information, analyze, think, and come to a conclusion using reason. "Decision" looks quite similar to "judgement." However, "decision" lies in "*Hara*;" "*Hara*" means "abdomen." In Japanese, this could mean mind, courage or heart."To judge," will be conducted by AI in the coming age, but "to decide" can be conducted only by humans. Therefore, management must be conducted by humans. The foundation of decision is based on learning. Experiences of establishing the enterprise and stock trading have been and will be helpful to nurture my decision making ability.

In the insurance industry, the Insurance Business Law was revised again in 2014, which made it stricter. For twenty years following the deregulation, the insurance industry has been full of over-competition for various companies attempting to enter the insurance field. However, Advance Create has employed a strategy to do business in the condition of almost no competitors, having shifted from store merchandising to an internet merchandising system in 2006. "Not to give up but to advance." From a viewpoint of risk management, it is risk to quit the store merchandising approach, which could generate profit. However, I decided to take a risk. I believe that my decision resulted in a good opportunity to avoid the hazard of excessive competition, which most insurance companies are confronted with today.

■ Enterprise Data

Advance Create Co., Ltd. https://www.advancecreate.co.jp/

Advance Create was established in 1995, was listed on NASDAQ Japan of Osaka Stock Exchange (the name at that time) in 2002, opened "*Hoken Ichiba*" in 2004, and concentrated on an internet merchandising system, and was listed on the second section of the Tokyo Stock Exchange in 2015. The next year, in 2016, Advance Create was listed on the first section of the Tokyo Stock Exchange.

2 Enthusiasm for business is the key to risk management
Ivresse Co., Ltd. Chief Executive Officer, Keiko Yamakawa

Ivresse Co., Ltd. engages in planning and producing custom-made products related to items placed in hotel and ryokan (Japanese-style inns) rooms, such as writing materials, and hotel amenities, and also producing interiors and equipment as a coordinator with designers and clients from the first stage. We have worked,

Interview 61

aiming to create luxury facilities with the approach of "*omotenashi*" and "*shitsurae*," which means "hospitality" and "installation of arrangements."

When we started this business, we had difficulties finding manufactures for our products in Japan. Expanding the target areas for manufactures to Asia, we found a production plant which was able to produce items of high quality, and we were enabled to pursue our ideal products. We provided sophisticated products to luxury hotels, city hotels and high-class Japanese style hotels, which increasingly started to do business with Ivresse. Finally, the brand value of Ivresse was raised.

I strongly believe that increasing the trust from clients is the best form of risk management, in performing a project. Ivresse does what only Ivresse can do.

One hotel has hundreds or thousands of business partners, depending on the scale of the hotel. Thus, a price war frequently happens due to competition. However, Ivresse would not compete on price to develop business. Fortunately, we have plentiful clients with a different sensitivity to price and quality. We appreciate the clients' consideration. Some clients make their way to our showroom and tell us that they would like to carry out planning as soon as possible. We also have other clients who truly agree with our suggestions. The clients treat us with passion and we respond with our full efforts and more passion than the clients. This is the corporate philosophy of Ivresse.

With times changing, trends are changing, the needs of hotel guests are changing, and the required functions of hotels are changing. We think that it is essential to promptly observe changes overtime, to learn incessantly, and to be flexible in responding to changes.

Ivresse has passed through many difficulties. The Great East Japan Earthquake in March of 2011, combined with the long-term appreciation of the yen, has had a massive impact on hotel industry. Guest-room occupancy rates were low for a long period. The number of bankruptcies was over one hundred in 2011, although the hotel industry had been in a severe economic condition before the earthquake struck (based on the research of Teikoku Databank, Ltd.).

The business results of hotels immediately influenced the business results of Ivresse. The amount sold in 2011 decreased by half in comparison to the previous year. We decided to leave issues of profit out of consideration to enthusiastically work together with our clients, who struggled to overcome adverse circumstances. Later, Tokyo was selected as a host city of the Summer Olympics in 2013, which had positive impacts on the hotel industry. Under these circumstances, Ivresse had great opportunities to work with new clients who manage "*shukuhaku-tokka-gata*" hotels, a no-frills hotel, for a specialized stay, but does not mean poor quality. We have learned diversified things in a new field with the eagerness of the clients, polishing ideas, and we are still business partners now. Most of the clients who opened a new hotel, gained an excellent reputation, as shown on online reservation sites for hotels.

Iversse recovered the amount sold one year after the Great East Japan Earthquake and later was doubled. At the same time, we reconsidered methods of foreign trade transactions and improved business structures to enhance stability.

We will keep the corporate philosophy "We do what only Ivresse can do." We will enhance our flexibility, taking the lead for the needs of clients in changing times and enthusiastically complete our task.

■ Enterprise Data

Ivresse Co., Ltd. http://www.ivresse.jp/

Ivresse was established in 1990. The headquarters is located in Chuo-ku, Osaka, Japan. Offices are located in Tokyo and Qingdao. Dozens of plants are affiliated domestically and overseas. Ivresse undertakes the production of hotel amenities and other items related to hotels, mainly by made-to-order production. With the expansion of business, producing total interiors and consulting on management are engaged in these days.

Fig. 9.1 Keiko Yamakawa, founder of Ivresse Co., Ltd.
at Kansai University Takatsuki Muse Campus (June 2017, photograph by Katsuyuki Kamei)

Exercise:

Choose one entrepreneur and describe one of his or her risk taking decisions.

Interview 63

Column 5: Business Succession in Wine Industry

Decision-making is required for business management succession; whom, when and how to succeed. Successors must make a decision of how they would respect the business approaches of the predecessor, and at the same time, how they would develop new businesses with the promotion of individuality and originality. Needless to say, these decisions entail grave risk of failure.

Robert Mondavi Winery (U.S.A.)

Mondavi's retreat from Languedoc, France project (2001) and its influences on the business succession. Robert Mondavi(1913-2008) has been called "the father of California wine" and increased the worldwide recognition of California wine from what was an obscure wine region. The business successions of the Mondavi winery were far from successful for Robert Mondavi, both from his father and to his sons, which were induced by family feuds. Evidently, both the predecessors and successors were lacking in mutual understanding and consideration.

"There has been repeated dissention between Robert Mondavi's three children… These family conflicts weakened the company to such an extent that the Constellation Brands group launched a hostile takeover bid in October, and succeeded in gaining control of the company."(Torrès, 2006, pp.151-152)

Mas de Daumas Gassac (France)

On the other hand, Aimé Guibert(1925-2016), who is well known for his fight against Mondavi's project, maintained good communication with his children, having a deep understanding of the situations of his children. Consequently, the business succession of Mas de Daumass Gassace was conducted smoothly.

Reference
Olivier TORRES, *The Wine Wars The Mondavi Affair, Globalization and 'Terroir'*, Palgrave, 2006.

Conclusion

As essential factors of decision-making and facing risks in a dilemma, a framework of risk management is shown below along with additional explanations of the items, which were mentioned in the introduction.

Risk; "*ri*" of "risk"	
Sakioku "ri-sk" 　Procrastinate	Postpone ⟷ Take a speedy action. Even when an effective measure is suggested, they do not introduce it, thinking an accident would not occur. They leave a risk without responding to opinions of coworkers or consumers. Focusing only on cost, they think they could not bear the cost, misjudging the value of the benefit. They leave the risk without consideration. They intentionally ignore the risk.
Tatewa "ri-sk" 　Vertical segment	Vertical segment system enables them to have an overall outlook ⟷ Build a horizontal connection. Lack of "Cross-functionality".
Itsuwa "ri-sk" 　Lying	To be caught lying ⟷ Disclosure before being pointed out from the outside. Criticism could be more damaging than it is supposed as, which could be worse than the defective event itself.
Miteminufu "ri-sk" 　Pretending not to see	Neglect; Seeing but pretending not to see ⟷ Accept the fact. A subordinate does not honestly report when an inappropriate fact is revealed. A supervisor turns a deaf ear.
Sakibashi "ri-sk" 　Get ahead of oneself	Action based on doubtful information ⟷ Treat the risk based on reliable assumption. Making a wrong decision without sufficient investigation in advance related to identification, analysis, and assessment of risks
Hitoriyoga "ri-sk" 　Self-satisfaction	Uncontrollable action of a dictatorial leader ⟷ He or she has to be admonished by a decisive "*bantoh*," who is a head clerk, and also a company culture which encourages anybody to speak out must be created. A risk of the manager, atmosphere where workers are discouraged from speaking out, and wrong decisions are made by a dictatorial leader
Hikikomo "ri-sk" 　Social withdrawl	A narrow view and lack of wide perspective ⟷ Have a wide range of view. Short-sighted manager, "Your commonness could not be applied to commonness in the world." Having knowledge only on one type of industry, which they belong to. Ignorance of situations of other companies or companies abroad
Ase "risk" 　Impatience	Impatience or being in a hurry ⟷ Response with composure. Losing countenance in sufficient time and information, when a risk is confronted

Risk Treatment; "ri" of "risupeikuto-respect"	
Tsunagari Connection	Respect the horizontal connection to redress harmful influences of vertical segment system. Respect open-minded human relations in the workplace, warmness and heart-warming actions.
Omoiyari Thoughtfulness	Respect the workers who make efforts on safety management and risk response. Respect employees who have a hard time due to uncontrollable actions or wrong decisions of a dictatorial leader
Dandori Course of action	Respect the accomplishment of process in identification, assessment, analysis and risk response.
Katari Narrative	Respect the communication concerning as follows; What risk the organization is confronted with How the organization will respond to the risk
Kaori and tezawari Aroma and feeling smooth	Respect the heeling effects on mental risk management

Index

Acceptance : 11
Active retention : 10
Advance Create Co. : 59, 60
AED : 48, 50, 51
Akemi Masuda : 49
Anti-terrorism : 52
Avoid : 29, 43
Avoidance : 10, 11
BCP : 6, 37, 38, 39, 40
Burge : 18, 21, 22
Business Succession : 23, 27
Carlos Ghosn : 43
Choice : i, 12
Citizen Marathon / Road Race
    Management Guideline : 48
Communication : i, 12
communication and consultation : 7
Coordination : i, 12, 13
Corporate Philosophy : 18
Crisis Management : 6, 15, 16, 17, 33
decision : i, ii, 2, 3, 6, 11, 12, 21, 22,
    23, 43, 45, 60, 65, 66
Denial : 20
Dilemma : 15
disease : 30, 31, 32, 49
Earth run club : 51, 52

Eisai Co. : 10, 13
Elimination : 10
Enterprise Risk Management (ERM) : 1
Entrepreneurial museum of challenge
    and innovation : 27
Entrepreneurs : 27
Espace : 43, 44, 45, 46
evacuation zones : 53
exposure : 4, 8
family business : 24, 25
Great East Japan Earthquake : 33, 37,
    38, 40, 61, 62
Great Hanshin Earthquake : 33
Hard Control : 11
Harry Potter Area : 46
hazard : 4, 30, 37, 60
Health Management : 29, 31, 32
Health Training Hall : 29, 30, 31
Hideko Oikawa : 34, 35
Hoken Ichiba : 59, 60
Hori kinhakufun : 25
Hori Metal Leaf & Powder : 25, 26, 27
Insurance : 6, 16, 30, 49, 59, 60
Interceptor Drone Team (IDT) : 53
International Organization for
    Standardization (ISO) 73 : 4

Ishinomaki Red Cross Hospital : 35
ISO3100:2018 : 7
JIS Q 31000:2019 : 7
ISO 31000 (2009, 2018) : 2
Establishing the context : 7
ISO 31000: 2018 : 7, 11
Isumi Kenkoh Marathon : 47, 49, 56
Ivresse : 60, 61, 62
Japan Association of Athletics
    Federations (JAAF) : 47, 48, 55
Johnson & Johnson : 17, 19, 21, 22
Kashiwa no ha marathon : 51
Kazuie Iinuma : 35
Keiko Yamakawa : 60, 62
Kesennuma : 35
Kumamoto Earthquake : 31, 37, 38, 39,
    40
Leadership : 6, 17, 33
loss : i, 3, 4, 6, 8, 9, 13, 20, 43
Loss Only Risk : 3
Loss or Gain Risk : 3
Louis Renault : 43
Marathon : 47, 48, 49, 51, 53, 56
Matra : 43, 44, 45
minivan : 43, 44
mitigation : 10, 11
monitoring and review : 7
Natural Disasters : 33, 37
Oikawa Denim : 34, 35
oral care : 29, 30, 31
Organization of Risk Management : 14
Osaka Marathon : 47, 51
Our Credo : 18, 19, 22
Passive retention : 10
peril : 4
Peter L. Bernstein : 2, 15
Pure Risk : 3
Peugeot : 43, 44, 45
Reducing a loss : 10
Removal : 11

Renault : 43, 44, 45, 46
Renesas Electronics Corporation : 38
Resilience : 6, 15
respect : i, 7, 13, 17, 19, 23, 55, 66
Retain : 11, 43
Retention : 10, 11
retreat : 59
risk : i, ii, 1, 2, 3, 4, 5, 6, 7, 8, 9, 10, 11,
    12, 13, 14, 15, 17, 19, 20, 21, 22,
    23, 24, 27, 29, 30, 31, 32, 33, 35,
    38, 40, 43, 44, 45, 46, 47, 48, 55,
    60, 61, 65, 66
Risk Assessment : 9
Risk Communication : 12
Risk Control : 10, 11
Risk Finance : 10, 11
Risk Identification : 8
risk management : i, ii, 1, 2, 3, 4, 6, 7, 8,
    9, 10, 11, 12, 13, 14, 15, 16, 19, 20,
    21, 22, 23, 24, 27, 29, 30, 31, 33,
    35, 37, 38, 40, 43, 45, 47, 48, 55,
    60, 61, 65, 66
Risk management in business
    succession : 24
Risk Management Process : 7
Risk Sensitivity : 2, 6
Risk Taking : 27, 43
Risk Treatment : i, 3, 6, 7, 10, 11, 12,
    24, 45
Safety Management : 6, 47, 51, 55
Sharing : 11
Shinise : 23, 27
Simulation training : 6
Small and Medium Enterprises : 2, 24
Social Responsibility : 18
social risk management : ii, 4, 54
Soft Control : 11
Sony Corporation : 39
Speculative Risk : 3, 45
Sunstar : 29, 30, 32

Index 69

Sunstar Mental and Physical Health
  Training Hall : 30
Technology, Entertainment, Design
  (TED) : 34
Tedlow : 20, 21, 22
TEDxTohoku : 33, 34, 36
Three aspects of risk : 9
Three "tei"s : 2
The Tokyo Marathon : 47, 52, 53, 54,
  55, 56

Tokyo Ohka Kogyo Co., Ltd. : 40
Tomoyuki Hori : 26
Toshiaki Kamei : 1
Transferring : 10, 11
Tylenol : 17, 18, 19, 20, 21
Tylenol Crisis : 17, 20
Universal Studio Japan : 46
Yoshiharu Hamada : 59
Zenji Katagata : 1

本書は以下の研究成果の一部である。

・2019 年度〜 2021 年度　文部科学省 科学研究費補助金 基盤研究(C) 19K11233
　中小企業経営者における職業性ストレスの尺度開発と実態解明の研究
・2017 年度〜 2019 年度　文部科学省 科学研究費補助金 基盤研究(C) 17K02374
　コンサートイベントのリスクマネジメントに関する理論的・実証的研究
・2018 年度〜 2019 年度　堺市と関西大学との地域連携事業「ホスピタルアート
　のある街」 堺のブランド力向上と堺市民の健康意識向上への貢献
・2016 年度〜 2017 年度　関西大学 国際交流助成基金による関西大学と協定大
　学間の共同研究助成（ルーベン・カトリック大学）中小企業の CSR と地域
　社会における変革マネジメント Corporate Social Responsibility of SMEs and
　Change Management at Community

・2015 年度〜 2018 年度　関西大学経済・政治研究所　スポーツ・健康と地域社
　会研究班

Report

Report

Author:

Katsuyuki KAMEI
Professor
PDM, Ph.D. of Disaster Management Program
Graduate School of Societal Safety Sciences
Kansai University
Osaka, Japan

Vice-president
Japan Risk Management Society

President
Société Franco-Japonaise de Gestion

Ph.D. Commerce,
Osaka City University Graduate School

DEA Sciences de Gestion
IAE d'Aix-en-Provence, Université Aix-Marseille III

Editing Support:

Progress International Inc.
Fukuoka, Japan

Cover illustration:

Konomi ASAHI
Berlin, Germany